CS-6   GENERAL APTITUDE AND ABILITIES SERIES

This is your
PASSBOOK for...

Civil Service Arithmetic

Test Preparation Study Guide
Questions & Answers

COPYRIGHT NOTICE

This book is SOLELY intended for, is sold ONLY to, and its use is RESTRICTED to individual, bona fide applicants or candidates who qualify by virtue of having seriously filed applications for appropriate license, certificate, professional and/or promotional advancement, higher school matriculation, scholarship, or other legitimate requirements of education and/or governmental authorities.

This book is NOT intended for use, class instruction, tutoring, training, duplication, copying, reprinting, excerption, or adaptation, etc., by:

1) Other publishers
2) Proprietors and/or Instructors of "Coaching" and/or Preparatory Courses
3) Personnel and/or Training Divisions of commercial, industrial, and governmental organizations
4) Schools, colleges, or universities and/or their departments and staffs, including teachers and other personnel
5) Testing Agencies or Bureaus
6) Study groups which seek by the purchase of a single volume to copy and/or duplicate and/or adapt this material for use by the group as a whole without having purchased individual volumes for each of the members of the group
7) Et al.

Such persons would be in violation of appropriate Federal and State statutes.

PROVISION OF LICENSING AGREEMENTS – Recognized educational, commercial, industrial, and governmental institutions and organizations, and others legitimately engaged in educational pursuits, including training, testing, and measurement activities, may address request for a licensing agreement to the copyright owners, who will determine whether, and under what conditions, including fees and charges, the materials in this book may be used them. In other words, a licensing facility exists for the legitimate use of the material in this book on other than an individual basis. However, it is asseverated and affirmed here that the material in this book CANNOT be used without the receipt of the express permission of such a licensing agreement from the Publishers. Inquiries re licensing should be addressed to the company, attention rights and permissions department.

All rights reserved, including the right of reproduction in whole or in part, in any form or by any means, electronic or mechanical, including photocopying, recording, or by any information storage and retrieval system, without permission in writing from the Publisher.

Copyright © 2024 by
National Learning Corporation

212 Michael Drive, Syosset, NY 11791
(516) 921-8888 • www.passbooks.com
E-mail: info@passbooks.com

PUBLISHED IN THE UNITED STATES OF AMERICA

PASSBOOK® SERIES

THE *PASSBOOK® SERIES* has been created to prepare applicants and candidates for the ultimate academic battlefield – the examination room.

At some time in our lives, each and every one of us may be required to take an examination – for validation, matriculation, admission, qualification, registration, certification, or licensure.

Based on the assumption that every applicant or candidate has met the basic formal educational standards, has taken the required number of courses, and read the necessary texts, the *PASSBOOK® SERIES* furnishes the one special preparation which may assure passing with confidence, instead of failing with insecurity. Examination questions – together with answers – are furnished as the basic vehicle for study so that the mysteries of the examination and its compounding difficulties may be eliminated or diminished by a sure method.

This book is meant to help you pass your examination provided that you qualify and are serious in your objective.

The entire field is reviewed through the huge store of content information which is succinctly presented through a provocative and challenging approach – the question-and-answer method.

A climate of success is established by furnishing the correct answers at the end of each test.

You soon learn to recognize types of questions, forms of questions, and patterns of questioning. You may even begin to anticipate expected outcomes.

You perceive that many questions are repeated or adapted so that you can gain acute insights, which may enable you to score many sure points.

You learn how to confront new questions, or types of questions, and to attack them confidently and work out the correct answers.

You note objectives and emphases, and recognize pitfalls and dangers, so that you may make positive educational adjustments.

Moreover, you are kept fully informed in relation to new concepts, methods, practices, and directions in the field.

You discover that you are actually taking the examination all the time: you are preparing for the examination by "taking" an examination, not by reading extraneous and/or supererogatory textbooks.

In short, this PASSBOOK®, used directedly, should be an important factor in helping you to pass your test.

CIVIL SERVICE ARITHMETIC

This book covers the types of questions generally asked on civil service, government, licensing and other exams, which may include some or all of the following areas:

1. Arithmetic concepts and computation;
2. Arithmetical reasoning;
3. Mathematics problem solving;
4. Mathematical relationships;
5. Measurement relationships and principles; and
6. Tables and formulae.

HOW TO TAKE A TEST

You have studied long, hard and conscientiously.

With your official admission card in hand, and your heart pounding, you have been admitted to the examination room.

You note that there are several hundred other applicants in the examination room waiting to take the same test.

They all appear to be equally well prepared.

You know that nothing but your best effort will suffice. The "moment of truth" is at hand: you now have to demonstrate objectively, in writing, your knowledge of content and your understanding of subject matter.

You are fighting the most important battle of your life—to pass and/or score high on an examination which will determine your career and provide the economic basis for your livelihood.

What extra, special things should you know and should you do in taking the examination?

I. YOU MUST PASS AN EXAMINATION

A. WHAT EVERY CANDIDATE SHOULD KNOW
Examination applicants often ask us for help in preparing for the written test. What can I study in advance? What kinds of questions will be asked? How will the test be given? How will the papers be graded?

B. HOW ARE EXAMS DEVELOPED?
Examinations are carefully written by trained technicians who are specialists in the field known as "psychological measurement," in consultation with recognized authorities in the field of work that the test will cover. These experts recommend the subject matter areas or skills to be tested; only those knowledges or skills important to your success on the job are included. The most reliable books and source materials available are used as references. Together, the experts and technicians judge the difficulty level of the questions.
Test technicians know how to phrase questions so that the problem is clearly stated. Their ethics do not permit "trick" or "catch" questions. Questions may have been tried out on sample groups, or subjected to statistical analysis, to determine their usefulness.
Written tests are often used in combination with performance tests, ratings of training and experience, and oral interviews. All of these measures combine to form the best-known means of finding the right person for the right job.

II. HOW TO PASS THE WRITTEN TEST

A. BASIC STEPS

1) Study the announcement

How, then, can you know what subjects to study? Our best answer is: "Learn as much as possible about the class of positions for which you've applied." The exam will test the knowledge, skills and abilities needed to do the work.

Your most valuable source of information about the position you want is the official exam announcement. This announcement lists the training and experience qualifications. Check these standards and apply only if you come reasonably close to meeting them. Many jurisdictions preview the written test in the exam announcement by including a section called "Knowledge and Abilities Required," "Scope of the Examination," or some similar heading. Here you will find out specifically what fields will be tested.

2) Choose appropriate study materials

If the position for which you are applying is technical or advanced, you will read more advanced, specialized material. If you are already familiar with the basic principles of your field, elementary textbooks would waste your time. Concentrate on advanced textbooks and technical periodicals. Think through the concepts and review difficult problems in your field.

These are all general sources. You can get more ideas on your own initiative, following these leads. For example, training manuals and publications of the government agency which employs workers in your field can be useful, particularly for technical and professional positions. A letter or visit to the government department involved may result in more specific study suggestions, and certainly will provide you with a more definite idea of the exact nature of the position you are seeking.

3) Study this book!

III. KINDS OF TESTS

Tests are used for purposes other than measuring knowledge and ability to perform specified duties. For some positions, it is equally important to test ability to make adjustments to new situations or to profit from training. In others, basic mental abilities not dependent on information are essential. Questions which test these things may not appear as pertinent to the duties of the position as those which test for knowledge and information. Yet they are often highly important parts of a fair examination. For very general questions, it is almost impossible to help you direct your study efforts. What we can do is to point out some of the more common of these general abilities needed in public service positions and describe some typical questions.

1) General information

Broad, general information has been found useful for predicting job success in some kinds of work. This is tested in a variety of ways, from vocabulary lists to questions about current events. Basic background in some field of work, such as sociology or economics, may be sampled in a group of questions. Often these are principles which have become familiar to most persons through exposure rather than through formal training. It is difficult to advise you how to study for these questions; being alert to the world around you is our best suggestion.

2) Verbal ability

An example of an ability needed in many positions is verbal or language ability. Verbal ability is, in brief, the ability to use and understand words. Vocabulary and grammar tests are typical measures of this ability. Reading comprehension or paragraph interpretation questions are common in many kinds of civil service tests. You are given a paragraph of written material and asked to find its central meaning.

IV. KINDS OF QUESTIONS

1. Multiple-choice Questions

Most popular of the short-answer questions is the "multiple choice" or "best answer" question. It can be used, for example, to test for factual knowledge, ability to solve problems or judgment in meeting situations found at work.

A multiple-choice question is normally one of three types:
- It can begin with an incomplete statement followed by several possible endings. You are to find the one ending which best completes the statement, although some of the others may not be entirely wrong.
- It can also be a complete statement in the form of a question which is answered by choosing one of the statements listed.
- It can be in the form of a problem – again you select the best answer.

Here is an example of a multiple-choice question with a discussion which should give you some clues as to the method for choosing the right answer:

When an employee has a complaint about his assignment, the action which will best help him overcome his difficulty is to
    A. discuss his difficulty with his coworkers
    B. take the problem to the head of the organization
    C. take the problem to the person who gave him the assignment
    D. say nothing to anyone about his complaint

In answering this question, you should study each of the choices to find which is best. Consider choice "A" – Certainly an employee may discuss his complaint with fellow employees, but no change or improvement can result, and the complaint remains unresolved. Choice "B" is a poor choice since the head of the organization probably does not know what assignment you have been given, and taking your problem to him is known as "going over the head" of the supervisor. The supervisor, or person who made the assignment, is the person who can clarify it or correct any injustice. Choice "C" is, therefore, correct. To say nothing, as in choice "D," is unwise. Supervisors have and interest in knowing the problems employees are facing, and the employee is seeking a solution to his problem.

2. True/False

3. Matching Questions

Matching an answer from a column of choices within another column.

V. RECORDING YOUR ANSWERS

Computer terminals are used more and more today for many different kinds of exams.

For an examination with very few applicants, you may be told to record your answers in the test booklet itself. Separate answer sheets are much more common. If this separate answer sheet is to be scored by machine – and this is often the case – it is highly important that you mark your answers correctly in order to get credit.

VI. BEFORE THE TEST

YOUR PHYSICAL CONDITION IS IMPORTANT

If you are not well, you can't do your best work on tests. If you are half asleep, you can't do your best either. Here are some tips:

1) Get about the same amount of sleep you usually get. Don't stay up all night before the test, either partying or worrying—DON'T DO IT!
2) If you wear glasses, be sure to wear them when you go to take the test. This goes for hearing aids, too.
3) If you have any physical problems that may keep you from doing your best, be sure to tell the person giving the test. If you are sick or in poor health, you relay cannot do your best on any test. You can always come back and take the test some other time.

Common sense will help you find procedures to follow to get ready for an examination. Too many of us, however, overlook these sensible measures. Indeed, nervousness and fatigue have been found to be the most serious reasons why applicants fail to do their best on civil service tests. Here is a list of reminders:

- Begin your preparation early – Don't wait until the last minute to go scurrying around for books and materials or to find out what the position is all about.
- Prepare continuously – An hour a night for a week is better than an all-night cram session. This has been definitely established. What is more, a night a week for a month will return better dividends than crowding your study into a shorter period of time.
- Locate the place of the exam – You have been sent a notice telling you when and where to report for the examination. If the location is in a different town or otherwise unfamiliar to you, it would be well to inquire the best route and learn something about the building.
- Relax the night before the test – Allow your mind to rest. Do not study at all that night. Plan some mild recreation or diversion; then go to bed early and get a good night's sleep.
- Get up early enough to make a leisurely trip to the place for the test – This way unforeseen events, traffic snarls, unfamiliar buildings, etc. will not upset you.
- Dress comfortably – A written test is not a fashion show. You will be known by number and not by name, so wear something comfortable.
- Leave excess paraphernalia at home – Shopping bags and odd bundles will get in your way. You need bring only the items mentioned in the official notice you received; usually everything you need is provided. Do not bring reference books to the exam. They will only confuse those last minutes and be taken away from you when in the test room.

- Arrive somewhat ahead of time – If because of transportation schedules you must get there very early, bring a newspaper or magazine to take your mind off yourself while waiting.
- Locate the examination room – When you have found the proper room, you will be directed to the seat or part of the room where you will sit. Sometimes you are given a sheet of instructions to read while you are waiting. Do not fill out any forms until you are told to do so; just read them and be prepared.
- Relax and prepare to listen to the instructions
- If you have any physical problem that may keep you from doing your best, be sure to tell the test administrator. If you are sick or in poor health, you really cannot do your best on the exam. You can come back and take the test some other time.

VII. AT THE TEST

The day of the test is here and you have the test booklet in your hand. The temptation to get going is very strong. Caution! There is more to success than knowing the right answers. You must know how to identify your papers and understand variations in the type of short-answer question used in this particular examination. Follow these suggestions for maximum results from your efforts:

1) Cooperate with the monitor

The test administrator has a duty to create a situation in which you can be as much at ease as possible. He will give instructions, tell you when to begin, check to see that you are marking your answer sheet correctly, and so on. He is not there to guard you, although he will see that your competitors do not take unfair advantage. He wants to help you do your best.

2) Listen to all instructions

Don't jump the gun! Wait until you understand all directions. In most civil service tests you get more time than you need to answer the questions. So don't be in a hurry. Read each word of instructions until you clearly understand the meaning. Study the examples, listen to all announcements and follow directions. Ask questions if you do not understand what to do.

3) Identify your papers

Civil service exams are usually identified by number only. You will be assigned a number; you must not put your name on your test papers. Be sure to copy your number correctly. Since more than one exam may be given, copy your exact examination title.

4) Plan your time

Unless you are told that a test is a "speed" or "rate of work" test, speed itself is usually not important. Time enough to answer all the questions will be provided, but this does not mean that you have all day. An overall time limit has been set. Divide the total time (in minutes) by the number of questions to determine the approximate time you have for each question.

5) Do not linger over difficult questions

If you come across a difficult question, mark it with a paper clip (useful to have along) and come back to it when you have been through the booklet. One caution if you do this – be sure to skip a number on your answer sheet as well. Check often to be sure that you have not lost your place and that you are marking in the row numbered the same as the question you are answering.

6) Read the questions

Be sure you know what the question asks! Many capable people are unsuccessful because they failed to read the questions correctly.

7) Answer all questions

Unless you have been instructed that a penalty will be deducted for incorrect answers, it is better to guess than to omit a question.

8) Speed tests

It is often better NOT to guess on speed tests. It has been found that on timed tests people are tempted to spend the last few seconds before time is called in marking answers at random – without even reading them – in the hope of picking up a few extra points. To discourage this practice, the instructions may warn you that your score will be "corrected" for guessing. That is, a penalty will be applied. The incorrect answers will be deducted from the correct ones, or some other penalty formula will be used.

9) Review your answers

If you finish before time is called, go back to the questions you guessed or omitted to give them further thought. Review other answers if you have time.

10) Return your test materials

If you are ready to leave before others have finished or time is called, take ALL your materials to the monitor and leave quietly. Never take any test material with you. The monitor can discover whose papers are not complete, and taking a test booklet may be grounds for disqualification.

VIII. EXAMINATION TECHNIQUES

1) Read the general instructions carefully. These are usually printed on the first page of the exam booklet. As a rule, these instructions refer to the timing of the examination; the fact that you should not start work until the signal and must stop work at a signal, etc. If there are any special instructions, such as a choice of questions to be answered, make sure that you note this instruction carefully.

2) When you are ready to start work on the examination, that is as soon as the signal has been given, read the instructions to each question booklet, underline any key words or phrases, such as least, best, outline, describe and the like. In this way you will tend to answer as requested rather than discover on reviewing your paper that you listed without describing, that you selected the worst choice rather than the best choice, etc.

3) If the examination is of the objective or multiple-choice type – that is, each question will also give a series of possible answers: A, B, C or D, and you are called upon to select the best answer and write the letter next to that answer on your answer paper – it is advisable to start answering each question in turn. There may be anywhere from 50 to 100 such questions in the three or four hours allotted and you can see how much time would be taken if you read through all the questions before beginning to answer any. Furthermore, if you

come across a question or group of questions which you know would be difficult to answer, it would undoubtedly affect your handling of all the other questions.

4) If the examination is of the essay type and contains but a few questions, it is a moot point as to whether you should read all the questions before starting to answer any one. Of course, if you are given a choice – say five out of seven and the like – then it is essential to read all the questions so you can eliminate the two that are most difficult. If, however, you are asked to answer all the questions, there may be danger in trying to answer the easiest one first because you may find that you will spend too much time on it. The best technique is to answer the first question, then proceed to the second, etc.

5) Time your answers. Before the exam begins, write down the time it started, then add the time allowed for the examination and write down the time it must be completed, then divide the time available somewhat as follows:
   - If 3-1/2 hours are allowed, that would be 210 minutes. If you have 80 objective-type questions, that would be an average of 2-1/2 minutes per question. Allow yourself no more than 2 minutes per question, or a total of 160 minutes, which will permit about 50 minutes to review.
   - If for the time allotment of 210 minutes there are 7 essay questions to answer, that would average about 30 minutes a question. Give yourself only 25 minutes per question so that you have about 35 minutes to review.

6) The most important instruction is to read each question and make sure you know what is wanted. The second most important instruction is to time yourself properly so that you answer every question. The third most important instruction is to answer every question. Guess if you have to but include something for each question. Remember that you will receive no credit for a blank and will probably receive some credit if you write something in answer to an essay question. If you guess a letter – say "B" for a multiple-choice question – you may have guessed right. If you leave a blank as an answer to a multiple-choice question, the examiners may respect your feelings but it will not add a point to your score. Some exams may penalize you for wrong answers, so in such cases only, you may not want to guess unless you have some basis for your answer.

7) Suggestions
   a. Objective-type questions
      1. Examine the question booklet for proper sequence of pages and questions
      2. Read all instructions carefully
      3. Skip any question which seems too difficult; return to it after all other questions have been answered
      4. Apportion your time properly; do not spend too much time on any single question or group of questions
      5. Note and underline key words – all, most, fewest, least, best, worst, same, opposite, etc.
      6. Pay particular attention to negatives
      7. Note unusual option, e.g., unduly long, short, complex, different or similar in content to the body of the question
      8. Observe the use of "hedging" words – probably, may, most likely, etc.

9. Make sure that your answer is put next to the same number as the question
10. Do not second-guess unless you have good reason to believe the second answer is definitely more correct
11. Cross out original answer if you decide another answer is more accurate; do not erase until you are ready to hand your paper in
12. Answer all questions; guess unless instructed otherwise
13. Leave time for review

b. Essay questions
   1. Read each question carefully
   2. Determine exactly what is wanted. Underline key words or phrases.
   3. Decide on outline or paragraph answer
   4. Include many different points and elements unless asked to develop any one or two points or elements
   5. Show impartiality by giving pros and cons unless directed to select one side only
   6. Make and write down any assumptions you find necessary to answer the questions
   7. Watch your English, grammar, punctuation and choice of words
   8. Time your answers; don't crowd material

8) Answering the essay question

Most essay questions can be answered by framing the specific response around several key words or ideas. Here are a few such key words or ideas:

M's: manpower, materials, methods, money, management
P's: purpose, program, policy, plan, procedure, practice, problems, pitfalls, personnel, public relations

a. Six basic steps in handling problems:
   1. Preliminary plan and background development
   2. Collect information, data and facts
   3. Analyze and interpret information, data and facts
   4. Analyze and develop solutions as well as make recommendations
   5. Prepare report and sell recommendations
   6. Install recommendations and follow up effectiveness

b. Pitfalls to avoid
1. Taking things for granted – A statement of the situation does not necessarily imply that each of the elements is necessarily true; for example, a complaint may be invalid and biased so that all that can be taken for granted is that a complaint has been registered
2. Considering only one side of a situation – Wherever possible, indicate several alternatives and then point out the reasons you selected the best one
3. Failing to indicate follow up – Whenever your answer indicates action on your part, make certain that you will take proper follow-up action to see how successful your recommendations, procedures or actions turn out to be
4. Taking too long in answering any single question – Remember to time your answers properly

EXAMINATION SECTION

ARITHMETIC

COMPUTATION AND REASONING

COMMENTARY

Practically every formal written examination - civil service, admission, matriculation, qualifying, promotion, aptitude, or achievement - attempts to measure, either directly or indirectly, the general aptitude of the candidate in two principal sectors of intelligence - qualitative (verbal) and quantitative (mathematical).

This section presents five (5) tests in arithmetic computation and reasoning - together with answers and solutions - designed to test and evaluate the quantitative (mathematical) aspect of intelligence of the applicant and to enable him to note and diagnose his strengths and weaknesses.

The best review of arithmetic fundamentals is to be effected by attempting the five (5) Tests that follow, consisting of 125 questions in all. These will enable you to engage in all the basic operations. The solutions, clearly and definitively portrayed, will take you, step-by-step, through each phase and aspect of the problem. This will constitute the most effective form of individualized learning on your part.

Arithmetic, together with reading, spelling and vocabulary, are basal parts of civil service examinations and tests of general and mental ability and aptitude. The material in this section, therefore, will prepare you not only for the present examination but for most of the examinations that you will eventually take.

Take each of the tests in arithmetic that follow. Then diagnose your shortcomings and failures by observing closely the solutions presented. In this way you will learn most surely and most confidently.

EXAMINATION SECTION
TEST 1

DIRECTIONS: Answer all questions. Each answer MUST be reduced to its simplest form.

SOLUTIONS APPEAR ON PAGE 3.

1. Add $43.50; $9.95; $7.98; $67.33.

2. Subtract .0879 from 3.0008.

3. Divide 474.32 by 56.

4. Add 3 1/4; 2 3/5; 5 1/2; 3 3/10

5. How many times greater than 6 kilometers is 36 kilometers?

6. Peter had 5 yards of lacing to cut into 20-in. pieces. How many pieces measuring exactly 20 in. each can he cut from the lacing?

7. At the rate of 50 cents per hundred pounds, how much did a license cost for an automobile weighing 3100 pounds?

8. Express 12 1/2% as a fraction.

9. If 9 eggs out of 12 hatched, what percent of the eggs hatched?

10. Which of the following is greater: 35 billion or 35 million?

11. If a discount of 20% is given on an article marked $17.50, what is the selling price?

12. One-half dozen eggs added to four eggs equals how many eggs?

13. If 3 packages of flavor make 1 quart of drink, how many packages will be needed to make one gallon?

14. At 80 cents an hour, how much will a boy earn in 5 hours and 15 minutes?

15. How much profit will be made on one gross of pencils if a profit of 1 cent is made on each pencil?

16. From 3 feet 6 inches subtract 1 foot 10 inches.

17. Each edge of a cube is 2 centimeters long. What is the volume of the cube?

18. How much tax must be paid on property assessed for $3800, if the tax rate is $15.65 per thousand?

19. If a = 4 and b = 6, what does 4a - b equal?

20. What percent of 16 is 8?

21. Find the area of a triangle having a base of 10 feet and an altitude of 8 feet.

22. If coal costs x dollars per ton, how much will 1/4 ton cost?

23. Find the circumference of a circle whose radius is 10 1/2 inches.

24. How much change should Jane get from a dollar when she buys 6 pounds of potatoes at 2 pounds for 9 cents?

25. Sam picked 36 baskets of apples, which he sold at 85 cents a basket. How much did he receive for the apples?

3 (#1)

SOLUTIONS TO PROBLEMS

1. $ 43.50
       9.75
       7.98
      67.33
    $128.76 [Ans.]

2.   3.0008
    - .0879
      2.9129 [Ans.]

3. $$56 \overline{)472.32} = 8.47 \text{ [Ans.]}$$
        448
        263
        224
        392
        392

4. 3 1/4   = 5/20
    2 3/5   = 12/20
    5 1/2   = 10/20
    3 3/10 = 6/20
    14 13/20 | 33/20 - 1 13/20
    [Ans.]

5. $\sqrt[6]{36} = 6$ [Ans.]

6. 1 yard = 36 inches

      36
      ×5
     180     $\sqrt[20]{180} = 9$ [Ans.]
                180

    5 yd. = 180 in.

7. $\sqrt[100]{3100} = 31$
     300
     100
     100

      31
    ×.50
    $15.50 [Ans.]

8.
$$12\ 1/2\% = \frac{12\frac{1}{2}}{100}$$

$$= 12\ 1/2 \div \frac{100}{1}$$

$$= \frac{\overset{1}{\cancel{25}}}{2} \times \frac{1}{\underset{4}{\cancel{100}}}$$

$$= 1/8 \ [Ans.]$$

9. $\dfrac{9}{12} = \dfrac{3}{4} = 75\%$ [Ans.]

10. 35 million = 35,000.000
    35 billion = 35,000,000,000
    35 billion is greater [Ans.]

11. $17.50 $17.50
     ×   .20   - 3.50
     ─────────   ─────────
     $3.5000 $14.00 [Ans.]

12. 1/2 doz. = 1/2 × 12 = 6
     6 + 4 = 10 [Ans.]

13. 1 gallon = 4 quarts
     3 × 4 = 12 [Ans.]

14. 15 minutes = $\dfrac{15}{60} = \dfrac{1}{4}$ hour

     $5\ 1/4 \times .80 = \dfrac{21}{\underset{1}{\cancel{4}}} \times \overset{.20}{\cancel{.80}}$

     = $4.20 [Ans.]

15. one gross = 144
     144 × .01 = $1.44 [Ans.]

16.   2   18
         $\cancel{3}$ ft. $\cancel{6}$ in.
     -   1 ft. 10 in.
         ─────────────
         1 ft. 8 in. [Ans.]

17. volume = length x width x height
     = 2 x 2 x 2
     = 8 cubic centimeters (or 8cc.)   [Ans.]

18.
$$1000\overline{)3800.0} = 3.8$$

$$\begin{array}{r} \$15.65 \\ \times\ \ 3.8 \\ \hline 12520 \\ 4695\ \ \\ \hline \$59470 \end{array}$$

$59.47 [Ans.]

19. 4a - b
     4x4 - 6
     16 - 6
     10 [Ans.]

20. $\frac{8}{16} = \frac{1}{2} = 50\%$ [Ans.]

21. A = 1/2 bh
     A = 1/2 10 8
     A = 40 sq. ft. [Ans.]

22. 1/4 ton costs
     $\frac{1}{4} \times$ or $\frac{x}{4}$ [Ans.]

23. c = 2πr
     $c = 2 \cdot \frac{22}{7} \cdot \frac{21}{2}$
     C = 66 inches [Ans.]

24. 2 pounds cost 9¢
     6 pounds cost 3 times as much
     3 x .09 = $.27

     $1.00
     - .27
     $ .73   [Ans.]

25.
     36
     x.85
     ───
     180
     288
     ───
     $30.60 [Ans.]

TEST 2

DIRECTIONS: Answer all questions. Each answer MUST be reduced to its simplest form.

SOLUTIONS APPEAR ON PAGE 5.

1. Find the sum of: .38; 4.01; 37; 24.3

2. Subtract 6 3/4 from 9 1/2

3. Divide 74.4 by .024

4. Find the product of 10,000 and .045

5. Which one of the following numbers has the smallest value: .2; .22; .02; .202; .022?

6. Write in figures: four and one-half million.

7. If a class of sixteen pupils going on a field trip has $8.00 to spend for lunches, how much money will each one be able to spend for lunch?

8. How many slices, each 1/4 in. thick, can be cut from an eighteen-inch piece of meat loaf?

9. After four pieces each 1 ft. 5 in. long were cut from a board, a piece 4 in. long remained. What was the original length of the board?

10. Write 2 1/2% as a decimal.

11. The scale of miles on a certain map is 1 inch = 50 miles. What is the distance in miles between two points that are 4 1/2 inches apart on the map?

12. An old-model electric toaster is marked at $22.50. If you receive a 10% discount on the marked price, what will you have to pay for the toaster?

13. An incubator hatched 558 chicks from 600 eggs. What percent of the eggs hatched?

14. What is the interest on a loan of $450 for 60 days at 6% interest?

15. A man invests $2000 and receives a yearly income of $100. What is the rate of income on his investment?

16. If the last day of school is Friday, June 22, and the first day of school in the fall is Tuesday, September 4, how many days are there in the vacation period?

17. What is the ratio of 6 feet to 3 feet?

18. One day 6% of the pupils enrolled in a school were absent. If 42 pupils were absent, how many pupils were enrolled in the school?

2 (#2)

19. The area of the floor of a square room is 144 feet. What is the length of one side of the floor?

20. How far above the earth, to the nearest mile, is a plane flying at an altitude of 15,000 feet?

21. If the perimeter of an equilateral triangle is 12 inches, what is the length of one side?

22. A man drove 80 miles in 2 hours and then 100 miles in 3 hours. What was his average speed for the 5 hours?

23. How many half-pint bottles can be filled with milk from a 10-gallon can of milk?

24. If y equals 6, what is the value of 3y - 4?

25. If a board is m inches long and a second board is 6 inches longer, what is the length of the second board in terms of m?

SOLUTIONS TO PROBLEMS

1.
   .38
   4.01
   37
   24.3
   ─────
   65.69 [Ans.]

2.
   8   =6 ft. [Ans.] or 72 in.
    1/2 = 2/4 + 4/4 = 6/4
   -6 3/4   = 3/4   - 3/4
   ─────   ─────
   2   9/4

         2 3/4 [Ans.]

3.
          3100
   .024) 74.400.   3100 [Ans.]
        72
        ──
         24
         24

4.
     10000
   × .045
   ──────
    50000
   40000
   ──────
   450.000 450 [Ans.]

5.
   .2 = .220 = 200/1000

   .22 = .220 = 220/1000

   .02 = .020 = 20/1000

   .202 = 202/1000

   .022 = 22/1000

   The number that has the smallest value is 20/100 or .02. [Ans.]

6. 1/2 million - 1/2 × 1,000,000 = 500,000
   4,500,000 [Ans.]

7.
       $ .50 [Ans.]
   16) $8.00
       80

4 (#2)

8. $18 \div 1/4$

   $18 \times \dfrac{4}{1} = 72$ [Ans.]

9. ```
   1 ft.  5 in.
   ×      4
   ─────────────
   4 ft. 20 in.
   +      4 in.
   ─────────────
   4 ft. 24 in.
   ```

10. $2\ 1/2\% = .02\ 1/2 = .025$ [Ans.]

11. $50 \times 4\ 1/2$

    $50 \times 9/2 = 450/2 = 225$ [Ans.]

12. ```
    $ 22.50              $22.50
         .10             -2.25
    ─────────           ───────
    2.25.00              $20.25 [Ans.]
    discount
    ```

13. $\dfrac{558}{600} = \dfrac{93}{100} = 93\%$

14. I-P × P × T

    $I = 450 \times \dfrac{6}{100} \times \dfrac{60}{360}$

    $I = 450 \times \dfrac{6}{100} \times \dfrac{1}{6} = \dfrac{450}{100}$

    I - $4.50 [Ans.]

15. $\dfrac{100}{20.00} = \dfrac{1}{20} \overline{)\begin{matrix}.05\\1.00\\1\ 00\end{matrix}}$

    .05 = 5% [Ans.]

16. ```
    June 23 - 30  inclusive =  8 da.
    July  1 - 31       "    = 31  "
    Aug.  1 - 31       "    = 31  "
    Sept. 1 -  3       "    =  3  "
                              ─────
                              73 da.
                              [Ans]
    ```

17. $\dfrac{6}{3} = \dfrac{2}{1}$ [Ans]

    or 2:1
    ```

5 (#2)

18. Let n = no. of pupils enrolled
.06n = 42
6 n = 4200
n = 700   [Ans.]

19. Let s = length of one side
of the floor
$s^2 = 144$
$s = \sqrt{144}$
$s = 12$ ft. [Ans.]

20.
```
          2.8  = 3 miles [Ans.]
    5280)15000.0
         10560
          44400
          42240
```

21. 1/3 x 12 = 4 inches [Ans.]

22. Average speed =
$\dfrac{\text{total distance}}{\text{total time}}$
$= \dfrac{180}{5}$
36 mph [Ans.]

23. 10 gallons = 40 quarts
= 80 pints
= 160 (half-pint bottles) [Ans.]

24. 3y - 4
3x6 - 4
18 - 4
14 [Ans.]

25. m + 6 [Ans.]

TEST 3

DIRECTIONS: Answer all questions. Each answer MUST be reduced to its simplest form.

SOLUTIONS APPEAR ON PAGE 8.

1. Add 736; 48; 402; 6389

2. Multiply 624 by 83 1/3

3. Add 5 3/4; 2 1/2; 9 3/8

4. Subtract $53.97 from $100

5. Divide 245.25 by 2.25

6. Divide 176 by 22/7

7. Which is larger: 42,000,000 or 42 billion?

8. A friend expected at 5:30 was 1 hour and 40 minutes late. At what time did he arrive?

9. Paul is 5 ft., 4 in. tall and Sam is 62 in. tall. Which boy is taller?

10. If you double the denominator of a fraction, do you increase or decrease the value of the fraction?

11. How much would you pay for 5 oranges at the rate of 60 cents a dozen?

12. On a three-hour bicycle trip a group of boys traveled 9 miles the first hour, 8 miles the second hour and 4 miles the third hour. How many miles per hour did the boys average?

13. If 14% of the stamps in a collection are domestic and the rest are foreign, what percent are foreign?

14. Jane sold Christmas cards for a total of $150. Of this she received $60 as a commission. What was the rate of commission on her sales?

15. A girl had 4 library books that were 3 days overdue. Her fine was 30 cents a day for each book. How much was her total fine?

16. Find the interest on $200 for 30 days if the rate of interest is 6%.

17. A year's subscription to a weekly magazine costs $9.75. If a single copy sells for 20 cents, how much will a person save by taking a year's subscription instead of buying a single copy each week?

18. A man owns property assessed at $7000. If the tax rate is $25 per $1000 this year, what is the amount of the tax on his property?

19. In one day an organization raised $60, which was 25% of its Red Cross quota. What was the organization's quota?

20. What measurement is indicated by the arrow on the 6-inch ruler pictured below?

21. Which has the larger area: a square with a side of 10 feet or a circle with a diameter of 10 feet?

22. What does 8^2 equal?

23. How many degrees are there in each angle of an equilateral triangle?

24. The product of two numbers is 120. If one of the numbers is 8, what is the other number?

25. What is the value of x in the equation 3x + 4 = 16?

SOLUTIONS TO PROBLEMS

1.
    ```
     736
      48
     402
    6389
    ----
    7575 [Ans.]
    ```

2.
    ```
       624
     ×83 1/3
     -------
       208
      1872
      4992
     -------
     $2,000 [Ans.]
    ```

3.
    ```
    5  3/4  =  6/8
    2  1/2  =  4/8
    9  3/8  =  3/8
    --             ----
    16        13/8  = 1 5/8
        16 + 1 5/8  = 17 5/8 [Ans.]
    ```

4.
    ```
    $100.00
    -  53.97
    --------
    $ 46.03 [Ans.]
    ```

5.
    ```
              109 [Ans.]
    2.25)245.25
         225
         ------
           20 25
           20 25
    ```

6. $176 \div \dfrac{22}{7}$

    $$\cancel{176}^{8} \times \dfrac{7}{\cancel{22}_{1}} = \dfrac{56}{1} = 56 \text{ [Ans.]}$$

    (cancel: 88, 176, 11, 1)

7. 42 billion = 42,000,000,000
   42 billion (is larger) [Ans.]

8.
    ```
     5:30
    +1:40
    -----
     6:70 = 7:10 [Ans.]
    ```

9. 5 ft., 4 in. = 60 + 4 = 64 in.
   Paul (is taller) [Ans.]

10. Take the fraction, 2/3.
    Doubling the denominator gives 2/6 = 1/3
    (You) decrease (the value of the fraction) [Ans.]

11. 5 oranges = 5/12 of a doz.
    5/12 x $.60 = $.25 or 25¢ [Ans.]

12. Average speed =
    $$\frac{\text{total distance}}{\text{total time}}$$

    Av. speed = $\frac{9+8+4}{3} = \frac{21}{3}$
    = 7 mph [Ans.]

13.
    ```
      100%
    -  14%
      86% [Ans.]
    ```

14. $\frac{60}{150} = \frac{2}{5} = 40\%$ [Ans.]

15. 4 x 30¢ = $1.20 fine each day
    $1.20 x 3 = $3.60 [Ans.]

16. I = P R T

    I = $200 × $\frac{6}{\cancel{100}}$ × $\frac{30}{\cancel{360}}$

    I = $\cancel{12}$ × $\frac{1}{\cancel{12}}$ = $1.00 [Ans.]

17.
    ```
        52           $10.40
       x.20         -  9.75
      $10.40         $ .65  [Ans.]
                    (or 65¢)
    ```

18.
    ```
           7          $25
    1000)7000         x  7
                     $175 [Ans.]
    ```

19. Let x = quota
    .25x = $60
    25x = 6000
       x = $240 [Ans.]

20. 2 5/8 inches [Ans.]

21. Area of square = 10 × 10 =
                            100 sq. ft.
    Area of circle = πr^2
                   = 3.14 × 5^2
                   = 3.14 × 25
                   = 78.5 sq. ft.
    (Area of) square (is larger) [Ans.]

22. 8^2 = 8 × 8 = 64 [Ans.]

23. Let x = each angle
    3x = 180°
     x = 60° [Ans.]

24. Let n = other number
    8n = 120
     n = 15 [Ans.]

25. 3x + 4 = 16
       - 4 = -4
       ―――――――
        3x = 12
         x = 4 [Ans.]

TEST 4

DIRECTIONS: Answer all questions. Each answer MUST be reduced to its simplest form.

SOLUTIONS APPEAR ON PAGE 11.

1. Find the sum of: 729, 803, 651

2. Multiply $.98 by 6 1/2

3. Divide 8 by 2/3

4. Divide 20.25 by .045

5. Add 6 7/8, 3 1/4, 2 1/2

6. Subtract 5 3/8 from 12

7. George and his father caught two fish that weighed 2 lb., 7 oz. and 4 lb., 15 oz. What was the total weight of the two fish?

8. Subtract 2 hours and 50 minutes from 5 hours and 12 minutes.

9. Rewrite 3,756,548 rounded off to the nearest thousand.

10. What percent of the figure at the right is shaded?

11. During a 33 1/3% discount sale, Jack's mother bought a chair that had originally been marked $45. How much did she save?

12. Express in dollars and cents the amount of money you would have if you had 5 quarters, 4 dimes, 6 nickels and 1 penny.

13. What is the interest on $600 for 8 months at 6%?

14. If a machine can print 3000 copies of a certain poster in 1 hour, how many minutes will it take, at the same rate of speed, for the machine to print 1000 copies?

15. If the school tax rate in a school district is $.02516 on each dollar of assessed valuation, what is the school tax on a piece of property having an assessed valuation of $1000?

16. In the pictogram at the right each complete figure represents 100,000 trees.
What is the total number of trees represented by the figures shown?

17. The weights of two anchors are in the ratio 2 to 3. If the smaller anchor weighs 50 pounds, what is the weight of the larger anchor?

18. One morning 2% of the pupils of a school were absent. If 16 pupils were absent, how many pupils were enrolled in the school?

19. What is the area of triangle ABE shown in the diagram if the dimensions of rectangle ABCD are 16 inches by 10 inches?

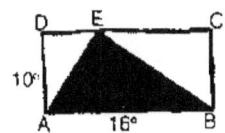

20. Express in terms of s the perimeter of the triangle at the right.

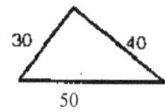

21. By what number do you multiply 9 in order to square it?

22. Name a line in the drawing at the right that represents a radius of the circle.

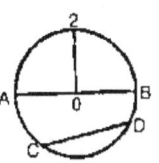

23. Write the following statement in the form of an equation:
If three times a certain number (x) is increased by 2, the result is 8.

24. Find the value of P in the formula P = 2m + 2w when m = 8 inches and w = 6 inches.

25. Solve the equation: 3x - 6 = 15

SOLUTIONS TO PROBLEMS

1. 729
    803
    651
    ―――
    2183 [Ans.]

2. $ .98   1/2 × 98 = 49
    × 6 1/2
    ―――――
       49
      588
    ―――――
    $6.37 [Ans.]

3. 8 ÷ 2/3 =
    8 × 3/2 = 12 [Ans.]

4.
    ```
              450
    .045)20.250
         18 0
         ―――
          2 25
          2 25
          ―――
    ```

5. 6 7/8   = 7/8
    3 1/4   = 2/8
    2 1/2   = 4/8
    ―――――――――――
    11   13/8 = 1 5/8
    11 + 1 5/8 = 12 5/8 [Ans.]

6.   11 8/8
     ~~12~~
    - 5 3/8
    ―――――――
      6 5/8 [Ans.]

7. 2 lb. 7 oz.
    4 lb. 15 oz.
    ――――――――――
    6 lb. 22 oz.   22 oz. = 1 lb., 6 oz.
    = 7 lb., 6 oz. [Ans.]

8.   4   72
     ~~5~~ hr. ~~12~~ min.
      2 hr. 50 min.
    ――――――――――――――
      2 hr., 22 min. [Ans.]

9. Since 548 is more
    than 1/2 of 1000,
    then 3,756.548
    becomes
    3,757,000 [Ans.]

4 (#4)

10. $\dfrac{10}{25} = \dfrac{2}{5} = 40\%$ [Ans.]

11. 1/3 of $45 = $15
    (discount)
    (She saved) $15 [Ans.]

12.
    5 quarters = 5 x .25 = $1.25
    4 dimes   = 4 x .10 =   .40
    6 nickels = 6 x .05 =   .30
    1 penny   = 1 x .01 =   .01
                           $ 1.96
                           [Ans.]

13. I = p × R × T
    $I = \$600 \times \dfrac{6}{100} \times \dfrac{8}{12}$
              12
    I = 36 × 2/3
    I = $24 [Ans.]

14. $\dfrac{1000}{3000} = \dfrac{1}{3}$

    $\dfrac{1}{3}$ of 1 hr. = $\dfrac{1}{3} \times 60$ min.

    = 20 min. [Ans.]

15. $1000 x .02516
    = $25.16 [Ans.]

16. 100,000 × 2 1/2
    $100{,}000 \times \dfrac{5}{2}$
    = 250,000 [Ans.]

17. Let x = weight of larger anchor

    $\dfrac{50}{x} = \dfrac{2}{3}$

    2x = 150
    x = 75 lb. [Ans.]

18. Let n = number of pupils enrolled
    .02n = 16
    2n   = 1600
    n   = 800 [Ans.]

19. The triangle has the same base and altitude as the rectangle.

    $A = \dfrac{1}{2} bh = \dfrac{1}{2} \times 16 \times 10$

    $A = 80$ sq. in. [Ans.]

20. $P = 3s + 4s + 5s$
    $P = 12s$ [Ans.]

21. $9^2 = 9 \times 9$
    9 [Ans.]

22. The radius may be represented by EO, AO, or BO [Ans.]

23. $3x + 2 = 8$ [Ans.]

24. $P = 2m + 2w$
    $P = 2 \times 8 + 2 \times 6$
    $P = 16 + 12$
    $P = 28$ inches [Ans.]

25. $3x - 6 = 15$
    $ +6\ \ +6$
    $\overline{3x\ \ = 21}$
    $x = 7$ [Ans.]

TEST 5

DIRECTIONS: Answer all questions. Each answer MUST be reduced to its simplest form.

SOLUTIONS APPEAR ON PAGE 15.

1. Find the value of 6 1/2 – 2 1/3 + 4 1/12

2. Subtract $4.98 from $10

3. Multiply 224 by 13 3/4

4. Divide 5.672 by .08

5. On a certain day the sun rises at 7:30 a. m. and sets at 5:15 p.m. How many hours and minutes is it from sunrise to sunset?

6. A ruler is placed against a metal plate as shown in the diagram. What is the length of the plate?

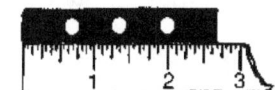

7. According to the census, a certain city had a population of 680,695. Write this number to the <u>nearest thousand</u>.

8. How many degrees are there in angle A of triangle ABC shown at the right?

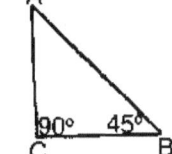

9. If a section 2 feet, 8 inches long is cut from a piece of lumber 10 feet long, what is the length of the part that remains?

10. The total cost of all food supplies needed for a camping trip for a group of Boy Scouts was $186. What was the cost of food for each one of the 20 Scouts who went on the trip?

11. If n represents a certain number, express in terms of n a number that is 3 less than 6 times n.

12. What percent of the figure at the right is shaded?

13. A class earned $60 commission from the sale of magazine subscriptions. This amount was equal to 25% commission on all sales. How many dollars worth of magazine subscriptions did they sell?

14. How many miles are represented by 2 1/4 inches on a map drawn to the scale 1 in. = 100 mi.?

15. The diameter of a circle is 28 inches. What is the circumference of the circle? (Use π = 3 1/7.)

16. The large rectangle at the right is made up of equal rectangles with dimensions as indicated. Express algebraically in terms of h and w the perimeter of the large rectangle.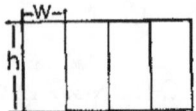

17. A boy is given a $100 bond that pays 2 3/4% interest annually. How much interest does he receive at the end of the first year?

18. A woman bought 12 yards of linen toweling. How many towels, each 27 inches long, can be cut from this length of material?

19. If n/3 = 4, what is the value of n?

20. The hypotenuse of a right triangle is 5 feet in length. One of the other sides of the triangle is 4 feet in length. What is the length of the third side?

21. The formula for finding the surface of a cube is $S = 6e^2$. Find S if e is 3 inches.

22. What amount of money is represented by the bar in the diagram below?

MILLIONS OF DOLLARS

Follow these directions in answering questions 23, 24 and 25: Choose the letter (a, b, c or d) representing the correct answer.

23. The fraction 2/3 has the same meaning as
     (a) 40% (b) 50% (c) 66 2/3% (d) 150%

24. Lines AD and AB of the rectangle pictured at the right are
     (a) equal (b) horizontal
     (c) parallel (d) perpendicular
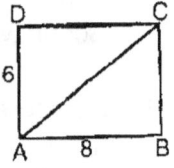

25. For which one of the following geometric solids is it possible to find the volume merely by multiplying its base by its height?

A.   B.    C.    D.

SOLUTIONS TO PROBLEMS

1. 6 1/2 - 2 1/3 + 4 1/12
   6 6/12 - 2 4/12 + 4 1/12
           4 2/12 + 4 1/12
           8 3/12 = 8 1/4 [Ans.]

2. $10.00
   - 4.98
   $ 5.02 [Ans.]

3.
   ```
        224
      × 13 3/4
      4)672
        168
        672
        224
      3,080  [Ans.]
   ```

4.
   ```
        70.9  [Ans.]
   .08./5.672
   ```

5. 7:30 a.m. to 5:15 p.m.

   7:30 to 12:00 = 4 hrs. 30 min.
   12:00 to 5:15 = 5 hrs. 15 min.
                    9 hrs. 45 min.
                        [Ans.]

6. 2 11/16 inches (Ans.)

7. 680,695
   681,000 [Ans.]

8.   90°
    -45°
     45° [Ans.]

9.
   ```
       9
      10 ft., 12 in.
     - 2 ft.,  8 in.
       7 ft.,  4 in.  [Ans.]
        or 7 1/3 ft.
   ```

10.
```
       9.30
   20)$186.00
      180
       60
       60
       00
```
$9.30 [Ans.]

11. 6n - 3 [Ans.]

12. 4/8 - 1/2 = 50% [Ans.]

13. Let x = number of dollars worth of subscriptions sold
25% x = 60
1/4 x   = 60
x   = $240   [Ans.]

14. 1 in. = 100 miles
2 1/4 in. = 100 x 2 1/4 or 225 miles   [Ans.]

15. $C = \pi b$
$C = 3\ 1/7 \times 28$
$= \dfrac{22}{7} \times 28 = 88$ in. [Ans.]

16. 8w + 2h <u>or</u> 2(4w + h) [Ans.]

17.
```
      $100
    x  2 3/4
    4)300
       75
      200
    $2.75  [Ans.]
```

18. 12 yds. = 432 in.

```
         16
    27)432
       27
       162
       162
           16 [Ans.]
```

19. n/3 = 4
n = 12 [Ans.]

20. Let x - length of 3rd side
$$x^2 + 4^2 = 5^2$$
$$x^2 + 16 = 25$$
$$-16 = -16$$
$$x^2 = 9$$
$$x = 3 \ [\text{Ans.}]$$

21.
$$8 = 6e^2$$
$$8 = 6 \times 9$$
$$8 = 54 \text{ sq. in.} \quad [\text{Ans.}]$$

22. $5,600,000 or
5.6 million dollars [Ans.]

23. 2/3 = 66 2/3%
(c) [Ans.]

24. AD and AB are perpendicular
(d) [Ans.]

25. Volume of cylinder = base x height
(c) [Ans.]

ARITHMETIC
EXAMINATION SECTION
TEST 1

DIRECTIONS: Each question or incomplete statement is followed by several suggested answers or completions. Select the one that *BEST* answers the question or completes the statement. *PRINT THE LETTER OF TEE CORRECT ANSWER IN THE SPACE AT THE RIGHT.*

1. Add $4.34, $34.50, $6.00, $101.76, $90.67. From the result, subtract $60.54 and $10,56.   1.____
   A. $76.17   B. $156.37   C. $166.17   D. $300.37

2. Add 2,200, 2,600, 252 and 47.96. From the result, subtract 202.70, 1,200, 2,150 and 434.43.   2.____
   A. 1,112.83   B. 1,213.46   C. 1,341.51   D. 1,348.91

3. Multiply 1850 by .05 and multiply 3300 by .08 and, then, add both results,   3.____
   A. 242.50   B. 264,00   C. 333.25   D. 356.50

4. Multiply 312.77 by .04. Round off the result to the nearest hundredth.   4.____
   A. 12.52   B. 12.511   C. 12.518   D. 12.51

5. Add 362.05, 91.13, 347.81 and 17.46 and then divide the result by 6. The answer, rounded off to the nearest hundredth, is: 5.____
   A. 138.409   B. 137.409   C. 136.41   D. 136.40

6. Add 66.25 and 15.06 and, then, multiply the result by 2 1/6. The answer is, most nearly,   6.____
   A. 176.18   B. 176.17   C. 162.66   D. 162.62

7. Each of the following items contains three decimals. In which case do *all* three decimals have the *SAME* value?   7.____
   A. .3; .30; .03
   C. 1.9; 1.90;1.09
   B. .25; .250; .2500
   D. .35; .350; .035

8. Add 1/2 the sum of (539.84 and 479.26) to 1/3 the sum of (1461.93 and 927.27). Round off the result to the nearest whole number.   8.____
   A. 3408   B. 2899   C. 1816   D. 1306

9. Multiply $5,906.09 by 15% and, then, divide the result by 3 and round off to the nearest cent.   9.____
   A. $295.30   B. $885.91   C. $2,657.74   D. $29,530.45

10. Multiply 630 by 517.   10.____
    A. 325,710   B. 345,720   C. 362,425   D. 385,660

29

11. Multiply 35 by 846.
    A. 4050   B. 9450   C. 18740   D. 29610

12. Multiply 823 by 0.05.
    A. 0.4115   B. 4.115   C. 41.15   D. 411.50

13. Multiply 1690 by 0.10.
    A. 0.169   B. .1.69   C. 16.90   D. 169.0

14. Divide 2765 by 35.
    A. 71   B. 79   C. 87   D. 93

15. From $18.55 subtract $6.80.
    A. $9.75   B. $10.95   C. $11.75   D. $25.35

16. The sum of 2.75 + 4.50 + 3.60 is:
    A. 9.75   B. 10.85   C. 11.15   D. 11.95

17. The sum of 9.63 + 11.21 + 17.25 is:
    A. 36.09   B. 38.09   C. 39.92   D. 41.22

18. The sum of 112.0 + 16.9 + 3.84 is:
    A. 129.3   B. 132.74   C. 136.48   D. 167.3

19. When 65 is added to the result of 14 multiplied by 13, the answer is:
    A. 92   B. 182   C. 247   D. 16055

20. From $391.55 subtract $273.45.
    A. $118.10   B. $128.20   C. $178.10   D. $218.20

KEY (CORRECT ANSWERS)

1.	C	11.	D
2.	A	12.	C
3.	D	13.	D
4.	D	14.	B
5.	C	15.	C
6.	B	16.	B
7.	B	17.	B
8.	D	18.	B
9.	C	19.	C
10.	A	20.	A

SOLUTIONS TO PROBLEMS

1. ($4.34 + $34.50 + $6.00 + $101.76 + $90.67) - ($60.54 + $10.56) = $237.27 - $71.10 = $166.17.

2. (2200 + 2600 + 252 + 47.96) - (202.70 + 1200 + 2150 + 434.43) = 5099.96 - 3987.13 = 1112.83

3. (1850)(.05) + (3300)(.08) = 92.5 + 264 = 356.50

4. (312.77)(.04) = 12.5108 = 12.51 to nearest hundredth

5. (362.05 + 91.13 + 347.81 + 17.46) ÷ 6 = 136.408$\overline{3}$ = 136.41 to nearest hundredth

6. (66.25 + 15.06)(2$\frac{1}{6}$) = 176.171$\overline{6}$ ≈ 176.17

7. .25 = .250 = .2500

8. ($\frac{1}{2}$)(539.84 + 479.26) + $\frac{1}{3}$(1461.93 + 927.27) = 509.55 + 796.4 = 1305.95 = 1306 nearest whole number

9. ($5906.09)(.15) ÷ 3 = ($885.9135)/3 = 295.3045 = $295.30 to nearest cent

10. (630)(517) = 325,710

11. (35)(846) = 29,610

12. (823)(.05) = 41.15

13. (1690)(10) = 169.0

14. 2765 ÷ 3.5 = 79

15. $18.55 - $6.80 = $11.75

16. 2.75 + 4.50 + 3.60 = 10.85

17. 9.63 + 11.21 + 17.25 = 38.09

18. 112.0 + 16.9 + 3.84 = 132.74

19. 65 + (14)(13) = 65 + 182 = 247

20. $391.55 - $273.45 = $118.10

TEST 2

DIRECTIONS   Each question or incomplete statement is followed by several suggested answers or completions. Select the one that BEST answers the question or completes the statement. PRINT THE LETTER OF TEE CORRECT ANSWER IN THE SPACE AT THE RIGHT.

1. The sum of $29.61 + $101.53 + $943.64 is: 1.____
   A. $983.88   B. $1074.78   C. $1174.98   D. $1341.42

2. The sum of $132.25 + $85.63 + $7056,44 is: 2.____
   A. $1694.19   B. $7274.32   C. $8464.57   D. $9346.22

3. The sum of 4010 + 1271 + 838 + 23 is: 3.____
   A.   6142   B.   6162   C.   6242   D.   6362

4. The sum of 53632 + 27403 + 98765 + 75424 is: 4.____
   A.   19214   B.   215214   C.   235224   D.   255224

5. The sum of 76342 + 49050 + 21206 + 59989 is: 5.____
   A.   196586   B.   206087   C.   206587   D.   234487

6. The sum of $452.13 + $963.45 + $621.25 is: 6.____
   A. $1936.83   B. $2036.83   C. $2095.73   D. $2135.73

7. The sum of 36392 + 42156 + 98765 is: 7.____
   A.   167214   B.   177203   C.   177313   D.   178213

8. The sum of 40125 + 87123 + 24689 is: 8.____
   A.   141827   B.   151827   C.   151937   D.   161947

9. The sum of 2379 + 4015 + 6521 + 9986 is: 9.____
   A.   22901   B.   22819   C.   21801   D.   21791

10. From 50962 subtract 36197.   10.____
    A.   14675   B.   14765   C.   14865   D.   24765

11. From 90000 subtract 31928.   11.____
    A.   58072   B.   59062   C.   68172   D.   69182

12. From 63764 subtract 21548.   12.____
    A.   42216   B.   43122   C.   45126   D.   85312

13. From $9605.13 subtract $2715.96.   13.____
    A. $12,321.09   B. $8,690.16   C. $6,990.07   D. $6,889.17

2 (#2)

14. From 76421 subtract 73101.   14.____
    A. 3642   B. 3540   C. 3320   D. 3242

15. From $8.25 subtract $6.50.   15.____
    A. $1.25   B. $1.50   C. $1.75   D. $2.25

16. Multiply 583 by 0.50.   16.____
    A. $291.50 B. 28.15   C. 2.815   D. 0.2815

17. Multiply 0.35 by 1045.   17.____
    A. 0.36575 B. 3.6575   C. 36.575   D. 365.75

18. Multiply 25 by 2513.   18.____
    A. 62825   B. 62725   C. 60825   D. 52825

19. Multiply 423 by 0.01.   19.____
    A. 0.0423   B. 0.423   C. 4.23   D. 42.3

20. Multiply 6.70 by 3.2.   20.____
    A. 2.1440   B. 21.440   C. 214.40   D. 2144.0

KEY (CORRECT ANSWERS)

1.	B	11.	A
2.	B	12.	A
3.	A	13.	D
4.	D	14.	C
5.	C	15.	C
6.	B	16.	A
7.	C	17.	D
8.	C	18.	A
9.	A	19.	C
10.	B	20.	B

3 (#2)

SOLUTIONS TO PROBLEMS

1. $29.61 + $101.53 + $943.64 = $1074.78

2. $132.25 + $85.63 + $7056.44 = $7274.32

3. 4010 + 1271 + 838 + 23 = 6142

4. 53,632 + 27,403 + 98,765 + 75,424 = 255,224

5. 76,342 + 49,050 + 21,206 + 59,989 = 206,587

6. $452.13 + $963.45 + $621.25 = $2036.83

7. 36,392 + 42,156 + 98,765 = 177,313

8. 40,125 + 87,123 + 24,689 = 151,937

9. 2379 + 4015 + 6521 + 9986 = 22,901

10. 50962 - 36197 = 14,765

11. 90,000 - 31,928 = 58,072

12. 63,764 - 21,548 = 42,216

13. $9605.13 - $2715.96 = $6889.17

14. 76,421 - 73,101 = 3320

15. $8.25 - $6.50 = $1.75

16. (583)(.50) = 291.50

17. (.35)(1045) = 365.75

18. (25)(2513) = 62,825

19. (423)(.01) = 4.23

20. (6.70)(3.2) = 21.44

TEST 3

DIRECTIONS: Each question or incomplete statement is followed by several suggested answers or completions. Select the one that *BEST* answers the question or completes the statement. *PRINT THE LETTER OF TEE CORRECT ANSWER IN THE SPACE AT THE RIGHT.*

Questions 1-4.

DIRECTIONS: For each of Questions 1-4, perform the indicated arithmetic and choose the correct answer from among the four choices given.

1. 12.485
   + 347

   A. 12,038 B. 12,128 C. 12,782 D. 12,832

   1._____

2. 74,137
   + 711

   A. 74,326 B. 74,848 C. 78,028 D. .D. 78,926

   2._____

3. 3,749
   - 671

   A. 3,078 B. 3,168 C. 4,028 D. 4,420

   3._____

4. 19,805
   -18904

   A. 109 B. 901 C. 1,109 D. 1,901

   4._____

5. When 119 is subtracted from the sum of 2016 + 1634, the remainder is:

   A. 2460 B. 3531 C. 3650 D. 3769

   5._____

6. Multiply 35 X 65 X 15.

   A. 2275 B. 24265 C. 31145 D. 34125

   6._____

7. 90% expressed as a decimal is:

   A. .009 B. .09 C. .9 D. 9.0

   7._____

8. Seven-tenths of a foot expressed in inches is:

   A. 5.5 B. 6.5 C. 7 D. 8.4

   8._____

9. If 95 men were divided into crews of five men each, the *number* of crews that will be formed is:

   A. 16 B. 17 C. 18 D. 19

   9._____

10. If a man earns $19.50 an hour, the *number* of working hours it will take him to earn $4,875 is, most nearly,

    A. 225 B. 250 C. 275 D. 300

11. If 5 1/2 loads of gravel cost $55.00, then 6 1/2 loads will cost:

    A. $60. B. $62.50 C. $65. D. $66.00

12. At $2.50 a yard, 27 yards of concrete will cost:

    A. $36. B. $41.80 C. $54. D. $67.50

13. A distance is measured and found to be 52.23 feet. In feet and inches, this distance is, most nearly, 52 feet *and*

    A. 2 3/4" B. 3 1/4" C. 3 3/4" D. 4 1/4"

14. If a maintainer gets $5.20 per hour and time and one-half for working over 40 hours, his *gross* salary for a week in which he worked 43 hours would be

    A. $208.00 B. $223.60 C. $231.40 D. $335.40

15. The circumference of a circle is given by the formula $C = \Pi D$, where C is the circumference, D is the diameter, and Π is about 3 1/7.
    If a coil is 15 turns of steel cable has an average diameter of 20 inches, the *total* length of cable on the coil is *nearest to*

    A. 5 feet B. 78 feet C. 550 feet D. 943 feet

16. The measurements of a poured concrete foundation show that 54 cubic feet of concrete have been placed.
    If payment for this concrete is to be on the basis of cubic yards, the 54 cubic feet must be

    A. multiplied by 27 B. multiplied by 3
    C. divided by 27   D. divided by 3

17. If the cost of 4 1/2 tons of structural steel is $1,800, then the cost of 12 tons is, most nearly,

    A. $4,800 B. $5,400 C. $7,200 D. $216,000

18. An hourly-paid employee working 12:00 midnight to 8:00 a.m. is directed to report to the medical staff for a physical examination at 11:00 a.m. of the same day.
    The pay allowed him for reporting will be an extra

    A. 1 hour B. 2 hours C. 3 hours D. 4 hours

19. The *total* length of four pieces of 2" pipe, whose lengths are 7' 3 1/2", 4' 2 3/16", 5' 7 5/16", and 8' 5 7/8", respectively, is:

    A. 24' 6 3/4"   B. 24' 7 15/16"
    C. 25' 5 13/16"   D. 25' 6 7/8"

20. As a senior mortuary caretaker, you are preparing a monthly report, using the following figures: 20.____

No. of bodies received	983
No. of bodies claimed	720
No. of bodies sent to city cemetery	14
No. of bodies sent to medical schools	9

    How many bodies remained at the end of the monthly reporting period?
    A. 230 B. 240 C. 250 D. 260

KEY (CORRECT ANSWERS)

1. D
2. B
3. A
4. B
5. B

6. D
7. C
8. D
9. D
10. B

11. C
12. D
13. A
14. C
15. B

16. C
17. A
18. C
19. D
20. B

SOLUTIONS TO PROBLEMS

1. 12,485 + 347 = 12,832

2. 74,137 + 711 = 74,848

3. 3749 - 671 = 3078

4. 19,805 - 18,904 = 901

5. (2016 + 1634) - 119 = 3650 - 119 = 3531

6. (35)(65)(15) = 34,125

7. 90% = .90 or .9

8. $(\frac{7}{10})(12) = 8.4$ inches

9. 95 ÷ 5 = 19 crews

10. $4875 ÷ $19.50 = 250 days

11. Let x = cost. Then, $\frac{5\frac{1}{2}}{6\frac{1}{2}} = \frac{\$55.00}{x}$. $5\frac{1}{2} = 357.50$. Solving, x = $65

12. ($2.50)(27) = $67.50

13. .23-ft. = 2.76 in., so 52.23 ft ≈ 52 ft. $2\frac{3}{4}$ in. $(.76 \approx \frac{3}{4})$

14. Salary = ($5.20)(40) + ($7.80)(3) = $231.40

15. Length ≈ $(15)(3\frac{1}{7})(20)$ ≈ 943 in. ≈ 78 ft.

16. There are 27 cu.ft. in 1 cu.yd. To change from 54 cu.ft. to cu.yds., divide by 27.

17. $1800 ÷ $4\frac{1}{2}$ = = $400 per ton. Then, 12 tons cost ($400)(12) = $4800

18. Instead of working 12 to 8, he will be staying until 11 AM, an extra 3 hours.

19. $7'3\frac{1}{2}" + 4'2\frac{3}{16}" + 5'7\frac{5}{16}" + 8'5\frac{7}{8}" = 24'17\frac{30}{16}" = 24'18\frac{7}{8}"$

20. 983 - 720 - 14 - 9 = 240 bodies left.

ARITHMETICAL COMPUTATION AND REASONING
EXAMINATION SECTION
TEST 1

DIRECTIONS: Each question or incomplete statement is followed by several suggested answers or completions. Select the one that BEST answers the question or completes the statement. *PRINT THE LETTER OF THE CORRECT ANSWER IN THE SPACE AT THE RIGHT.*

1. 3/8 less than $40 is
   A. $25   B. $65   C. $15   D. $55

2. 27/64 expressed as a percent is
   A. 40.625%   B. 42.188%   C. 43.750%   D. 45.313%

3. 1/6 more than 36 gross is _____ gross.
   A. 6   B. 48   C. 30   D. 42

4. 15 is 20% of

5. The number which when increased by 1/3 of itself equals 96 is
   A. 128   B. 72   C. 64   D. 32

6. 0.16 3/4 written as percent is
   A. 16 3/4%   B. 16.3/4%   C. .016 3/4%   D. .0016 3/4%

7. 55% of 15 is
   A. 82.5   B. 0.825   C. 0.0825   D. 8.25

8. The number which when decreased by 1/3 of itself equals 96 is
   A. 64   B. 32   C. 128   D. 144

9. A carpenter used a board 15 3/4 ft. long from which 3 footstools were made with sufficient lumber left over for half of another footstool.
   If the lumber cost 24 1/2¢ per foot, the cost of EACH footstool was
   A. $1.54   B. $3.86   C. $1.10   D. $1.08

10. In one year, a luncheonette purchased 1231 gallons of milk for $907.99. The AVERAGE cost per half pint was
    A. $0.046   B. $0.045   C. $0.047   D. $0.044

11. The product of 23 and 9 3/4 is
    A. 191 2/3   B. 224 1/4   C. 213 3/4   D. 32 3/4

12. An order for 345 machine bolts at $4.15 per hundred will cost
    A. $0.1432   B. $1.1432   C. $14.32   D. $143.20

13. The fractional equivalent of .0625 is

    A. 1/16   B. 1/15   C. 1/14   D. 1/13

14. The number 0.03125 equals

    A. 3/64   B. 1/16   C. 1/64   D. 1/32

15. 21.70 divided by 1.75 equals

    A. 124   B. 12.4   C. 1.24   D. .124

16. The average cost of school lunches for 100 children varied as follows: Monday, $0.285; Tuesday, $0.237; Wednesday, $0.264; Thursday, $0.276; Friday, $0.292. The AVERAGE lunch cost

    A. $0.136   B. $0.270   C. $0.135   D. $0.271

17. The cost of 5 dozen eggs at $8.52 per gross is

    A. $3.50   B. $42.60   C. $3.55   D. $3.74

18. 410.07 less 38.49 equals

    A. 372.58   B. 371.58   C. 381.58   D. 382.68

19. The cost of 7 3/4 tons of coal at $20.16 per ton is

    A. $15.12   B. $151.20   C. $141.12   D. $156.24

20. The sum of 90.79, 79.09, 97.90, and 9.97 is

    A. 277.75   B. 278.56   C. 276.94   D. 277.93

KEY (CORRECT ANSWERS)

1. A   11. B
2. B   12. C
3. D   13. A
4. C   14. D
5. B   15. B

6. A   16. D
7. D   17. C
8. D   18. B
9. C   19. D
10. A   20. A

SOLUTIONS TO PROBLEMS

1. ($40)(5/8) = $25

2. 27/64 = .421875 ≈ 42.188%

3. (36)(1 1/6) = 42

4. Let x = missing number. Then, 15 = .20x. Solving, x = 75

5. Let x = missing number. Then, x + 1/3 x = 96. Simplifying, 4/3 x = 96. Solving, x = 96 ÷ 4/3 = 72

6. .16 3/4 = 16 3/4% by simply moving the decimal point two places to the right.

7. (.55)(15) = 8.25

8. Let x = missing number. Then, x - 1/3 x = 96. Simplifying, 2/3 x = 96. Solving, x = 96 ÷ 2/3 = 144

9. 15 3/4 ÷ 3 1/2 = 4.5 feet per footstool. The cost of one footstool is ($.245)(4.5) = $1.1025 ≈ $1.10

10. $907.99 ÷ 1231 = $.7376 per gallon. Since there are 16 half-pints in a gallon, the average cost per half-pint is $.7376 ÷ 16 ≈ $.046

11. (23)(9 3/4) = (23)(9.75) = 224.25 or 224 1/4

12. ($4.15)(3.45) = $14.3175 = $14.32

13. .0625 = 625/10,000 = 1/16

14. .03125 = 3125/100,000 = 1/32

15. 21.70 ÷ 1.75 = 12.4

16. The sum of these lunches is $1.354. Then, $1.354 ÷ 5 = $.2708 = $.271

17. $8.52 ÷ 12 = $.71 per dozen. Then, the cost of 5 dozen is ($.71)(5) = $3.55

18. 410.07 - 38.49 = 371.58

19. ($20.16)(7.75) = $156.24

20. 90.79 + 79.09 + 97.90 + 9.97 = 277.75

TEST 2

DIRECTIONS: Each question or incomplete statement is followed by several suggested answers or completions. Select the one that BEST answers the question or completes the statement. *PRINT THE LETTER OF THE CORRECT ANSWER IN THE SPACE AT THE RIGHT.*

1. 1600 is 40% of what number?   1.____
   A. 6400   B. 3200   C. 4000   D. 5600

2. An executive's time card reads: Arrived 9:15 A.M., Left 2:05 P.M.   2.____
   How many hours was he in the office? _____ hours _____ minutes.
   A. 5; 10   B. 4; 50   C. 4; 10   D. 5; 50

3. .4266 times .3333 will have the following number of decimals in the product: 3.____
   A. 8   B. 4   C. 1   D. None of these

4. An office floor is 25 ft. wide by 36 ft. long.   4.____
   To cover this floor with carpet will require _____ square yards.
   A. 100   B. 300   C. 900   D. 25

5. 1/8 of 1% expressed as a decimal is   5.____
   A. .125   B. .0125   C. 1.25   D. .00125

6. $\dfrac{6 \div 4}{6 \times 4}$ equals 6x4   6.____
   A. 1/16   B. 1   C. 1/6   D. 1/4

7. 1/25 of 230 equals   7.____
   A. 92.0   B. 9.20   C. .920   D. 920

8. 4 times 3/8 equals   8.____
   A. 1 3/8   B. 3/32   C. 12.125   D. 1.5

9. 3/4 divided by 4 equals   9.____
   A. 3   B. 3/16   C. 16/3   D. 16

10. 6/7 divided by 2/7 equals   10.____
    A. 6   B. 12/49   C. 3   D. 21

11. The interest on $240 for 90 days ' 6% is   11.____
    A. $4.80   B. $3.40   C. $4.20   D. $3.60

12. 16 2/3% of 1728 is   12.____
    A. 91   B. 288   C. 282   D. 280

13. 6 1/4% of 6400 is
   A. 2500   B. 410   C. 108   D. 400

14. 12 1/2% of 560 is
   A. 65   B. 40   C. 50   D. 70

15. 2 yards divided by 3 equals
   A. 2 feet   B. 1/2 yard   C. 3 yards   D. 3 feet

16. A school has 540 pupils. 45% are boys. How many girls are there in this school?
   A. 243   B. 297   C. 493   D. 394

17. .1875 is equivalent to
   A. 18 3/4   B. 75/18   C. 18/75   D. 3/16

18. A kitchen cabinet listed at $42 is sold for $33.60. The discount allowed is
   A. 10%   B. 15%   C. 20%   D. 30%

19. 3 6/8 divided by 8 1/4 equals
   A. 9 1/8   B. 12   C. 5/11   D. 243.16

20. An agent sold goods to the amount of $1480. His commission at 5 1/2% was
   A. $37.50   B. $81.40   C. 76.70   D. $81.10

KEY (CORRECT ANSWERS

1. C
2. B
3. A
4. A
5. D

6. A
7. B
8. D
9. B
10. C

11. D
12. B
13. D
14. D
15. A

16. B
17. D
18. C
19. C
20. B

3 (#2)

SOLUTIONS TO PROBLEMS

1. Let x = missing number. Then, 1600 = .40x. Solving, x = 4000

2. 2:05 PM - 9:15 AM = 4 hours 50 minutes

3. The product of two 4-decimal numbers is an 8-decimal number.

4. (25 ft)(36 ft) = 900 sq.ft. = 100 sq.yds.

5. (1/8)(1%) = (.125)(.01) = .00125

6. (6 ÷ 4) ÷ (6 x 4) = 3/2 ÷ 24 = (3/2)(1/24)= (1/16)

7. (1/25)(230) = 9.20

8. (4)(3/8) = 12/8 = 1.5

9. 3/4 ÷ 4 = (3/4)(1/4) = 3/16

10. 6/7 / 2/7 = (6/7)(7/2) = 3

11. ($240)(.06)(90/360) = $3.60

12. (16 2/3%)(1728) = (1/6)(1728) = 288

13. (6 1/4%)(6400) = (1/16)(6400) = 400

14. (12 1/2%)(560) = (1/8)(560) = 70

15. 2 yds ÷ 3 = 2/3 yds = (2/3)(3) = 2 ft.

16. If 45% are boys, then 55% are girls. Thus, (540)(.55) = 297

17. .1875 = 1875/10,000 = 3/16

18. $42 - $33.60 = $8.40.
    The discount is $8.40 ÷ $42 = .20 = 20%

19. 3 6/8 - 8 1/4 = (30/8)(4/33) = 5/11

20. ($1480)(.055) = $81.40

TEST 3

DIRECTIONS: Each question or incomplete statement is followed by several suggested answers or completions. Select the one that BEST answers the question or completes the statement. *PRINT THE LETTER OF THE CORRECT ANSWER IN THE SPACE AT THE RIGHT.*

1. 93.648 divided by 0.4 is

    A. 23.412 B. 234.12 C. 2.3412 D. 2341.2

    1.____

2. Add 4.3682, .0028, 34., 9.92, and from the sum subtract 1.992. The remainder is

    A. .46299 B. 4.6299 C. 462.99 D. 46.299

    2.____

3. At $2.88 per gross, three dozen will cost

    A. $8.64 B. $0.96 C. $0.72 D. $11.52

    3.____

4. 13 times 2.39 times 0.024 equals

    A. 745.68 B. 74.568 C. 7.4568 D. .74568

    4.____

5. A living room suite is marked $64 less 25 percent. A cash discount of 10 percent is allowed.
   The cash price is

    A. $53.20 B. $47.80 C. $36.00 D. $43.20

    5.____

6. 1/8 of 1 percent expressed as a decimal is

    A. .125 B. .0125 C. 1.25 D. .00125

    6.____

7. 16 percent of 482.11 equals

    A. 77.1376 B. 771.4240 C. 7714.2400 D. 7.71424

    7.____

8. A merchant sold a chair for $60. This was at a profit of 25 percent of what it cost him.
   The chair cost him

    A. $48 B. $45 C. $15 D. $75

    8.____

9. Add 5 hours 13 minutes, 3 hours 49 minutes, and 14 minutes. The sum is _____ hours _____ minutes.

    A. 9; 16 B. 9;76 C. 8;16 D. 8;6

    9.____

10. 89 percent of $482 is

    A. $428.98 B. $472.36 C. $42.90 D. $47.24

    10.____

11. 200 percent of 800 is

    A. 16 B. 1600 C. 2500 D. 4

    11.____

12. Add 2 feet 3 inches, 4 feet 11 inches, 8 inches, 6 feet 6 inches.
    The sum is _____ feet _____ inches.

    A. 12; 4 B. 12; 14 C. 14; 4 D. 14; 28

    12.____

13. A merchant bought dresses at $15 each and sold them at $20 each. His overhead expenses are 20 percent of cost. His net profit on each dress is

    A. $1   B. $2   C. $3   D. $4

14. 0.0325 expressed as a percent is

    A. 325%   B. 3 1/4%   C. 32 1/2%   D. 32.5%

15. Add 3/4, 1/8, 1/32, 1/2; and from the sum subtract 4/8. The remainder is

    A. 2/32   B. 7/8   C. 29/32   D. 3/4

16. A salesman gets a commission of 4 percent on his sales. If he wants his commission to amount to $40, he will have to sell merchandise totaling

    A. $160   B. $10   C. $1,000   D. $100

17. Jones borrowed $225,000 for five years at 3 1/2 percent. The annual interest charge was

    A. $1,575   B. $1,555   C. $7,875   D. $39,375

18. A kitchen cabinet listed at $42 is sold for $33.60. The discount allowed is _____ percent.

    A. 10   B. 15   C. 20   D. 30

19. The exact number of days from May 5, 2007 to July 1, 2007 is _____ days.

    A. 59   B. 58   C. 56   D. 57

20. A dealer sells an article at a loss of 50% of the cost. Based on the selling price, the loss is

    A. 25%   B. 50%   C. 100%   D. none of these

KEY (CORRECT ANSWERS)

1.	B		11.	B
2.	D		12.	C
3.	C		13.	B
4.	D		14.	B
5.	D		15.	C
6.	D		16.	C
7.	A		17.	C
8.	A		18.	C
9.	A		19.	D
10.	A		20.	C

SOLUTIONS TO PROBLEMS

1. 93.648 ÷ .4 = 234.12

2. 4.368 + .0028 + 34 + 9.92 - 1.992 = 48.291 - 1.992 = 46.299

3. $2.88 for 12 dozen means $.24 per dozen. Three dozen will cost (3)($.24) = $.72

4. (13)(2.39)(.024) = .74568

5. ($64)(.75)(.90) = $43.20

6. (1/8)(1%) = (.125)(.01) = .00125

7. (.16)(482.11) = 77.1376

8. Let x = cost. Then, $1.25x = \$60$. Solving, $x = \$48$

9. 5 hrs. 13 min. + 3 hrs. 49 min. + 14 min = 8 hrs. 76 min.

10. (.89)($482) = $428.98

11. 200% = 2. So, (200%)(800) = (2)(800) = 1600

12. 2 ft. 3 in. + 4 ft. 11 in. + 8 in. + 6 ft. 6 in. + 12 ft. 28 in. = 14 ft. 4 in.

13. Overhead is (.20)($15) = $3. The net profit is $20 - $15 - $3 = $2

14. .0325 = 3.25% = 3 1/4%

15. 3/4 + 1/8 + 1/32 + 1/2 - 4/8 = 45/32 - 4/8 = 29/32

16. Let x = sales. Then, $\$40 = .04x$. Solving, $x = \$1000$

17. Annual interest is ($225,000)(.035) x 1 = 7875

18. $42 - $33.60 = $8.40. Then, $8.40 ÷ $42 = .20 = 20%

19. The number of days left for May, June, July is 26, 30, and 1. Thus, 26 + 30 + 1 = 57

20. Let x = cost, so that $.50x$ = selling price. The loss is represented by $.50x \div .50x = 1 = 100\%$ on the selling price. (Note: The loss in dollars is $x - .50x = .50x$)

BASIC MATHEMATICS
EXAMINATION SECTION
TEST 1

DIRECTIONS: Each question or incomplete statement is followed by several suggested answers or completions. Select the one that BEST answers the question or completes the statement. *PRINT THE LETTER OF THE CORRECT ANSWER IN THE SPACE AT THE RIGHT.*

1.   534
      18
  +1291

   A. 1733   B. 1743   C. 1833   D. 1843   E. 1853

1.____

2. (17×23) – 16 + 20 =
   A. 459   B. 427   C. 411   D. 395   E. 355

2.____

3. 3/7 + 5/11 =
   A. 33/35   B. 4/9   C. 8/18   D. 68/77   E. 15/77

3.____

4. 4832 ÷ 6 =
   A. 905 1/3   B. 805 1/3   C. 95 1/3   D. 95   E. 85 1/3

4.____

5. 62.3 – 4.9 =
   A. 5.74   B. 7.4   C. 57.4   D. 58.4   E. 67.4

5.____

6. 3/5 × 4/9 =
   A. 4/15   B. 7/45   C. 27/20   D. 12/14   E. 15/4

6.____

7. 14/16 – 5/16 =
   A. 8/16   B. 9/16   C. 11/16   D. 8   E. 9

7.____

8. 5.03 + 2.7 + 40 =
   A. .570   B. 4.773   C. 5.70   D. 11.73   E. 47.73

8.____

9. 5.37 × 21.4 =
   A. 11491.8   B. 1149.18   C. 114.918
   D. 11,4918   E. 1.14918

9.____

10. 5 1/4 + 2 7/8 =
   A. 8 1/4   B. 8 1/8   C. 7 2/3   D. 7 1/4   E. 7 1/8

10.____

11. -14 + 5 =
   A. -19   B. -9   C. 9   D. 19   E. 70

11.____

12. 2/7 of 28 =
    A. 98 B. 16 C. 14 D. 8 E. 4

13. 2/5 =
    A. .10 B. .20 C. .25 D. .40 E. .52

14. 20% of _____ is 38.
    A. 7.6 B. 19 C. 76 D. 190 E. 760

15. $\frac{8.4}{400}$ =
    A. .0021 B. .021 C. .21 D. 2.1 E. 21

16. $\frac{4}{5} = \frac{?}{60}$
    A. 240 B. 48 C. 20 D. 15 E. 12

17. What is the area of the rectangle shown at the right?
    A. 47 mm²
    B. 94 mm²
    C. 240 mm²
    D. 480 mm²
    E. 960 mm²

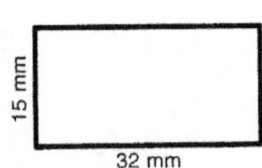

18. What number does ☐ represent in the following equation: 25 − ☐ ☐ ☐ ☐ = 13?
    A. 13 B. 12 C. 7 D. 4 E. 3

19. Approximate lengths are given in the right triangles shown at the right. What does length x equal?
    A. 48
    B. 39
    C. 37
    D. 35
    E. 32

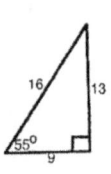 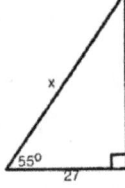

20. What is the perimeter of the triangle shown at the right?
    A. 10 × 15 × 17
    B. 10 + 15 + 17
    C. 1/2 × 10 × 15
    D. 1/2 × 10 × 17
    E. 1/2(10+15+17)

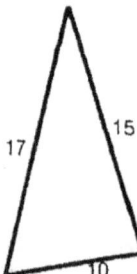

21. Which of the following expressions will give the same answer as 45 × 9?
    A. 5 × 3³ B. (4×9)+(5×9) C. (40+9) × 5
    D. (45×3) + (45×3) E. (45×10) − (45×1)

22. Find the average of 19, 21, 21, 22, and 27.
    A. 23   B. 22   C. 21   D. 20   E. 19

23. In the triangle at the right, how many degrees is <T?
    A. 75°
    B. 85°
    C. 95°
    D. 114°
    E. 180°

24. About how long is the paper clip?
    A. 5 cm   B. 4 cm   C. 3 cm   D. 2 cm   E. 1 cm

25. Five stores sell the same size cans of tomato soup. Their prices are listed below.
    Which sells the soup for the LOWEST price per can? _____ cans for _____.
    A. 6; 99¢   B. 6; 90¢   C. 5; 93¢   D. 3; 56¢   E. 3; 50¢

26. Rock star Peter Giles receives $1.97 royalty on each of his albums that is sold. 14,127 albums are sold.
    Estimate how much Peter Giles will receive.
    A. $7,000   B. $14,000   C. $20,000   D. $26,000   E. $28,000

27. An amplifier is advertised for 20% off the list price of $430. What is the sale price?
    A. $516   B. $454   C. $354   D. $344   E. $215

28. If 9 dozen eggs cost $3.60, what do 25 dozen eggs cost?
    A. $90.00   B. $10.00   C. $9.00   D. $2.54   E. $40

29. The distance between New York State and San Antonio is 1,860 miles. If a jet averages 465 miles per hour, how many hours will it take to travel the distance?
    A. 9   B. 5   C. 4   D. 3   E. 2

30. In a high school homeroom of 32 students, 24 are girls. What percent are girls?
    A. 3/4%   B. 24%   C. 25%   D. 75%   E. 80%

31. Which problem could give the answer shown on the calculator?
    A. 2 + .3
    B. 2 × 3/10
    C. 2 × 1/3
    D. 33333 + .2
    E. 7 ÷ 3

    `2.33333`

32. Cost of Eating at Home
    (One Week)

Age	Male	Female
6-11 yrs.	$14	$14
12-19 yrs.	$19	$15
20-54 yrs.	$20	$16
55 and Up	$14	$14

    According to the above table, how much will it cost in a typical week for the 3 members of the Wright family to eat at home? Mr. Wright is 56 years old; Mrs. Wright, 52; and their son, Harry, 17.
    A. $125   B. $52   C. $49   D. $42   E. $40

33. According to the above table shown in Question 32, how much does it cost in a typical four-week month to feed a 12-year-old girl?
    A. $4   B. $16   C. $48   D. $64   E. $78

34. Reverend Whilhite jogs for 1½ hours each day, 6 days a week.
    If he burns 800 calories per hour of jogging, how many calories does he burn in a week?
    A. 4800   B. 5600   C. 7200   D. 8400   E. 9000

35. Ground meat costs 90¢ per pound.
    How much does the meat on the scale cost?
    A. $1.80
    B. $1.60
    C. $1.54
    D. $1.44
    E. $.90

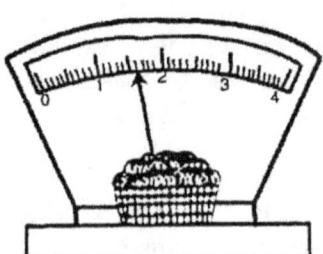

36. According to the graph at the right, about when did the weekly wages for a minimum wage worker go over $100?
    A. 2005
    B. 2010
    C. 2014
    D. 2019
    E. 2020

36.____

37. According to the bar graph at the right, what is the approximate height of the Crystal Beach Comet?
    A. 40 ft.
    B. 90 ft.
    C. 92 ft.
    D. 94 ft.
    E. 98 ft.

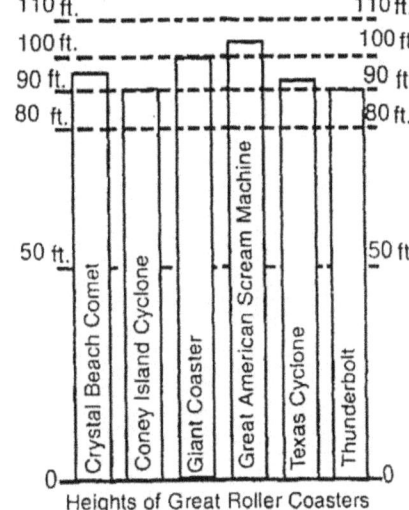

37.____

38. According to the bar graph shown in Question 37, what is the difference in height between the tallest and shortest roller coasters? _____ feet.
    A. 5   B. 10   C. 15   D. 20   E. 50

38.____

39. How much change will you receive from a $10 bill when you buy 4 grapefruits at 90¢ each and 3 apples at 40¢ each?
    A. $6.20   B. $5.20   C. $4.80   D. $4.20   E. $4.00

39.____

40. A medical supplier packages medicine in boxes. The cost of packaging is computed with the flow chart at the right.
What is the cost of packaging medicine in a box that is 30 cm long, 20 cm wide, and 20 cm high?
   A. $.20
   B. $.24
   C. $2.00
   D. $2.40
   E. $3.00

40.____

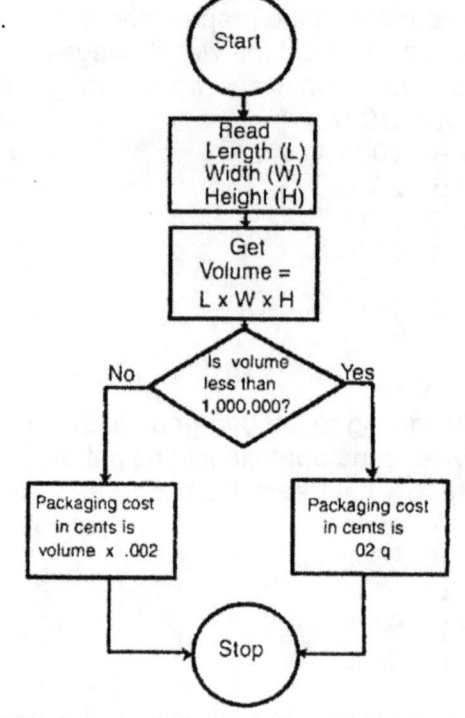

KEY (CORRECT ANSWERS)

1.	D	11.	B	21.	E	31.	E
2.	D	12.	D	22.	B	32.	C
3.	D	13.	D	23.	B	33.	D
4.	B	14.	D	24.	C	34.	C
5.	C	15.	B	25.	B	35.	D
6.	A	16.	B	26.	E	36.	C
7.	B	17.	D	27.	D	37.	D
8.	E	18.	E	28.	B	38.	C
9.	C	19.	A	29.	C	39.	B
10.	B	20.	B	30.	D	40.	A

7 (#1)

SOLUTIONS TO PROBLEMS

1. 534 + 18 + 1291 = 1843

2. (17×23) − 16 + 20 = 391 − 16 + 20 = 395

3. $\frac{3}{7} + \frac{5}{11} = \frac{33}{77} + \frac{35}{77} = \frac{68}{77}$

4. $4832 \div 6 = 805\frac{1}{3}$

5. 62.3 − 4.9 = 57.4

6. $\frac{3}{5} \times \frac{4}{9} = \frac{12}{45} = \frac{4}{15}$

7. $\frac{14}{16} \cdot \frac{5}{16} = \frac{9}{16}$

8. 5.03 + 2.7 + 40 = 47.73

9. 5.37 × 21.4 = 114.918

10. $5\frac{1}{4} + 2\frac{7}{8} = 7\frac{9}{8} = 8\frac{1}{8}$

11. -14 + 5 = -9

12. $\frac{2}{7}$ of 28 = $(\frac{2}{7})(\frac{28}{1})$ = 8

13. $\frac{2}{5}$ = .40 as a decimal

14. Let x = missing number. Then, .20x = 38. Solving, x = 190

15. $\frac{84}{400}$ = .021

16. Let x = missing number. Then, $\frac{4}{5} = \frac{x}{60}$. 5x = 240, so x = 48

17. Area = (15)(32) = 480mm^2

18. Let x = □. Then, 25 − 4x = 13. So, -4x = -12. Solving, x = 3.

19. $\frac{9}{27} = \frac{16}{x}$. Then, 9x = 432. Solving, x = 48.

20. Perimeter = 17 + 10 + 15 = 42

21. 45 × 9 = 405 = (45×10)-(45×1)

22. 19 + 21 + 21 + 22 + 27 = 110. Then, 110 ÷ 5 = 22

23. ∠T = 180° - 50° - 45° = 85°

24. The paper clip's length is about 5 – 2 = 3 cm.

25. For A: price per can = $\frac{.99}{6}$ = .165
    For B: price per can = $\frac{.90}{6}$ = .15
    For C: price per can = $\frac{.93}{5}$ = 186
    For D: price per can = $\frac{.56}{3}$ = .18$\overline{6}$
    For E: price per can = $\frac{.50}{3}$ = .1$\overline{6}$

    Lowest price is for B.

26. $1.97 ≈ $2.00. Then, ($2.00)(14,127) = $28,254 ≈ $28,000

27. Sale price = ($430)(.80) = $344

28. Let x = cost. Then, 9x = $90, so x = $10.00

29. $\frac{1860}{465}$ = 4 hours

30. $\frac{24}{32}$ = 75%

31. $\frac{7}{3}$ = 2.$\overline{3}$ = 2.33333 on the calculator shown

32. Total cost = $14 + $16 + $19 = $49

33. Cost = ($16)(4) = $64

34. (800)(1$\frac{1}{2}$)(6) = 7200 calories

35. (.90)(1.6) = $1.44

36. Around 2015, the minimum weekly wages exceeded $100.

37. The Crystal Beach Comet's height is about 94 ft.

38. Tallest = 105 ft. and the shortest = 90 ft. Difference = 15 ft.

39. $10 – (3)(.90) – (3)(.40) = $5.20 change.

40. (30)(20)(20) = 12,000 cm³. Since 12,000 < 1,000,000, the price is 20 cents.

ARITHMETICAL REASONING
EXAMINATION SECTION
TEST 1

DIRECTIONS: Each question or incomplete statement is followed by several suggested answers or completions. Select the one that BEST answers the question or completes the statement. *PRINT THE LETTER OF THE CORRECT ANSWER IN THE SPACE AT THE RIGHT.*

1. Assume that it takes approximately 1 1/2 minutes to unload a dozen identical items from a delivery truck.
   At this speed, the amount of time it should take to unload a shipment of 876 items is, MOST NEARLY, _____ minutes.
   A. 90   B. 100   C. 110   D. 120

2. Assume that a shop clerk has received a bill of $108 for a delivery of clamps which cost $4.32 per dozen.
   How many clamps should there be in this delivery?
   A. 25   B. 36   C. 300   D. 360

3. Employee A has not used any leave time and has accumulated a total of 45 leave-days.
   How many months did it take employee A to have accumulated 45 leave-days if the accrual rate is 1 2/3 days per months?
   A. 25   B. 27   C. 29   D. 31

4. A shop clerk is notified that only 75 bolts can be supplied by Vendor A.
   If this represents 12.5% of the total requisition, then how many bolts were originally ordered?
   A. 125   B. 600   C. 700   D. 900

5. An enclosed square-shaped storage area with sides of 16 feet each has a safe-load capacity of 250 pounds per square foot.
   The MAXIMUM evenly distributed weight that can be stored in this area is _____ lbs.
   A. 1,056   B. 4,000   C. 64,000   D. 102,400

6. A clerical employee completed 70 progress reports the first week, 87 the second week, and 80 the third week.
   Assuming a 4-week month, how many progress reports must the clerk complete in the fourth week in order to attain an average of 85 progress reports per week for the month?
   A. 93   B. 103   C. 113   D. 133

7. On the first of the month, Shop X received a delivery of 150 gallons of lubricating oil. During the month, the following amounts of oil were used on lubricating work each week: 30 quarts, 36 quarts, 20 quarts, and 48 quarts.
The amount of lubricating oil remaining at the end of the month was _____ gallons.
   A. 4   B. 33.5   C. 41.5   D. 116.5

7._____

8. For working a 35-hour week, Employee A earns a gross amount of $160.30. For each hour that Employee A works over 40 hours a week, he is entitled to 1 1/2 times his hourly wage rate.
If Employee A worked 9 hours on Monday, 8 hours on Tuesday, 9 hours 30 minutes on Wednesday, 9 hours 15 minutes on Thursday, and 9 hours 15 minutes on Friday, what should his gross salary be for that week?
   A. $206.10   B. $210.68   C. $217.55   D. $229.00

8._____

9. An enclosed cube-shaped storage bay has dimensions of 12 feet by 12 feet by 12 feet. Standard procedure requires that there be at least 1 foot of space between the walls, the ceiling and the stored items.
What is the MAXIMUM number of cube-shaped boxes with length, width, and height of 1 foot each that can be stored on 1-foot high pallets in this bay?
   A. 1,000   B. 1,331   C. 1,452   D. 1,728

9._____

10. Assume that two ceilings are to be painted. One ceiling measures 30 feet by 15 feet and the second 45 feet by 60 feet.
If one quart of paint will cover 60 square feet of ceiling, approximately how much paint will be required to paint the two ceilings?
   A. 6 gallons   B. 10 gallons   C. 13 gallons   D. 18 gallons

10._____

KEY (CORRECT ANSWERS)

1. C   6. B
2. C   7. D
3. B   8. C
4. B   9. A
5. C   10. C

SOLUTIONS TO PROBLEMS

1. 876 ÷ 12 = 73. Then, (73)(1 1/2) = 109.5 ≈ 110 minutes.

2. $108 ÷ $4.32 = 25. Then, (25)(12) = 300 clamps.

3. 45 ÷ 1 1/2 = 27 months

4. 75 ÷ .125 = 600 bolts

5. (16)(16)(250) == 64,000 pounds

6. (85)(4) = 340. Then, 340 – 70 – 87 – 80 = 103 progress reports.

7. Changing every calculation to gallons, the amount of oil remaining is 150 – 7.5 – 9 – 5 – 12 = 116.5.

8. 9 + 8 + 9.5 + 9.25 + 9.25 = 45 hours. His gross pay will be ($4.58)(40) + ($6.87)(5) = $217.55. (Note: To get his regular hourly wages, divide $160.30 by 35.)

9. 12 – 1 – 1 =10. Maximum number of boxes is $(10)^3$ = 1000.

10. First ceiling contains (30)(15) = 450 sq.ft., whereas the second ceiling contains (45)(60) = 2700 sq.ft. The total sq.ft. = 3150. Now, 3150 ÷ 60 = 52.5 quarts of paint = 13.125 or 13 gallons.

TEST 2

DIRECTIONS: Each question or incomplete statement is followed by several suggested answers or completions. Select the one that BEST answers the question or completes the statement. *PRINT THE LETTER OF THE CORRECT ANSWER IN THE SPACE AT THE RIGHT.*

1. A piping sketch is drawn to a scale of 1/8" = 1 foot.
   A vertical steam line measuring 3/4" on the sketch would have an actual length of _____ feet.
   A. 16   B. 22   C. 24   D. 28

   1._____

2. Three lengths of pipe 1'10", 3'2 1/2", and 5'7 1/2", respectively, are to be cut from a pipe 14'0" long.
   Allowing 1/8" for each pipe cut, the length of pipe remaining is
   A. 3'1 1/8"   B. 3'2 1/2"   C. 3'3 1/2"   D. 3'3 5/8"

   2._____

3. Assume that a steamfitter's helper earns $11.16 an hour and that he works 250 seven-hour days a year.
   His gross yearly salary will be
   A. 19,430   B. $19,530   C. $19,650   D. $19,780

   3._____

4. A pipe having an inside diameter of 3.48 inches and a wall thickness of .18 inches, will have an outside diameter of _____ inches.
   A. 3.84   B. 3.64   C. 3.57   D. 3.51

   4._____

5. A rectangular steel bar having a volume of 30 cubic inches, a width of 2 inches, and a height of 3 inches will have a length of _____ inches.
   A. 12   B. 10   C. 8   D. 5

   5._____

6. A pipe weighs 20.4 pounds per foot of length.
   The total weight of eight pieces of this pipe with each piece 20 feet in length is MOST NEARLY _____ pounds.
   A. 460   B. 1680   C. 2420   D. 3260

   6._____

7. In last year's budget, $7,500 was spent for office supplies. Of this amount, 60% was spent for paper supplies.
   If the price of paper has risen 20% over last year's price, then the amount that will be spent this year on paper supplies, assuming the same quantity will be purchased, will be
   A. $3,600   B. $5,200   C. $5,400   D. $6,000

   7._____

8. If it takes 4 painters 54 days to do a certain paint job, then the time it should take 5 painters working at the same speed to do the same job is MOST NEARLY _____ days.
   A. 3 1/2   B. 4   C. 4 1/2   D. 5

   8._____

9. A foreman assigns a gang foreman to supervise a job which must be completed at the end of 7 working days. The gang foreman has 8 maintainers in his gang. At the end of 3 working days, although the work has been efficiently done, the job is only one-third completed.
In order to complete the job on time, without overtime, the gang foreman should request that he be given _____ more maintainers.
   A. 3   B. 4   C. 5   D. 6

10. One shipment of 70 shovels costs $140. A second shipment of 130 shovels costs $208.00.
The average cost per shovel for both shipments is MOST NEARLY
   A. $1.60   B. $1.75   C. $2.00   D. $2.50

KEY (CORRECT ANSWERS)

1.	D	6.	D
2.	D	7.	C
3.	B	8.	C
4.	A	9.	B
5.	D	10.	B

SOLUTIONS TO PROBLEMS

1. 3 1/2 ÷ 1/8 = 28 feet.

2. 14' − 1'10" − 3' 1/2" − 5'7 1/2" − 1/8" − 1/8" − 1/8" = 3'3 5/8"

3. (250)(7) = 1750 hours. Then, ($11.16)(1750) = $19,530

4. Outside diameter = 3.48 + .18 + .18 = 3.84 inches

5. Length is 30 ÷ 2 ÷ 3 = 5 inches

6. (20)(8) = 160 feet. Then, (160)(20.4) = 3264 ≈ 3260 pounds

7. ($7,500)(.60) = $4,500. Then, ($4,500)(1.20) = $5,400

8. Let x = required days. Since this is an inverse ratio, 4/5 = x/5 1/2. Then, 5x = 22. Solving, x = 4.4 ≈ 4 1/2

9. (8)(3) = 24 man-days were needed to complete 1/3 of the job.
Since 2/3 of the job remains, the foreman will need 48 man-days for the remaining 4 days. This requires 12 men. Since he has 8 currently, he will need 4 more workers.

10. Average cost per shovel is ($140 + $208) ÷ (70+130) = $1.74, which is closest to $1.75.

TEST 3

DIRECTIONS: Each question or incomplete statement is followed by several suggested answers or completions. Select the one that BEST answers the question or completes the statement. *PRINT THE LETTER OF THE CORRECT ANSWER IN THE SPACE AT THE RIGHT.*

1. Assume that your warehouse received a shipment of 600 articles. A sample of 60 articles was inspected. Of this sample, one article was wholly defective and four articles were partly defective.
   On the basis of this sampling, you would expect the total number of defective articles in this shipment to be
   A. 5   B. 10   C. 40   D. 50

   1.____

2. Assume that you have been instructed to order mineral spirits as soon as the supply-on-hand falls to the level required for sixty days of issue.
   If the total amount of mineral spirits on hand is 960 gallons and you issue an average of 8 gallons of mineral spirits per day, and your warehouse works a five-day week, you will be required to order mineral spirits in _____ working days.
   A. 50   B. 60   C. 70   D. 80

   2.____

3. Assume that you work in a one-story warehouse where the total available floor space measures 175 feet by 140 feet. Of this floor space, one area measuring 35 feet by 75 feet is used for storing materials handling equipment, another area is measuring 10 feet by 21 feet is used for office space, and the remaining floor space is available for storage.
   The amount of floor space available for storage in this one-story warehouse is _____ square feet.
   A. 21,665   B. 21,875   C. 24,290   D. $24,500

   3.____

4. Assume that linoleum tiles measuring 9 inches by 9 inches are packed ten to a box and each box costs $3.50.
   The cost of buying enough linoleum tiles to cover an area measuring 15 feet by 21 feet is
   A. $98.00   B. $110.25   C. $196.00   D. $220.50

   4.____

5. The number of boxes measuring 3 inches by 3 inches by 3 inches that will fit into a carton measuring 2 feet by 4 feet is
   A. 2,048   B. 2,645   C. 7,936   D. 23,808

   5.____

6. The stock inventory card for paint, white, flat, one-gallon, has the following entries:

Date	Received	Shipped	Balance
April 12	-	25	75
April 13	50	75	
April 14	-	10	
April 15	25		
April 16			

   6.____

63

The balance on hand at the close of business on April 15 should be
A. 40   B. 45   C. 55   D. 65

7. The cost of one dozen pieces of screening, each measuring 4 feet 6 inches at $.10 per square foot is
A. $22.50   B. $25.00   C. $27.00   D. $27.60

8. Assume that it takes an average of ten man-hours to stack four tons of a particular item.
In order to stack 80 tons, the number of men required to complete the job in twenty hours is
A. 10   B. 20   C. 30   D. 40

9. Assume that you are required to relocate 5,000 reams of unboxed paper using only manual labor. The average time required for one laborer to pick 12 reams, carry them to the new location, and store them properly is ten minutes.
In order to complete this relocation task within one working day of seven hours, the MINIMUM number of laborers you should assign to this task is
A. 10   B. 15   C. 24   D. 70

10. Assume that you receive a shipment of 9 boxes of paper towels. Each box contains 6 dozen packages. Each package contains 200 paper towels. The total cost of the shipment of boxes is $64.80. The unit of issue for paper towels is the package.
The unit cost of the paper towels is
A. $.10   B. $.90   C. $1.20   D. $7.20

KEY (CORRECT ANSWERS)

1.	D	6.	D
2.	B	7.	C
3.	A	8.	A
4.	C	9.	A
5.	A	10.	A

3 (#3)

SOLUTIONS TO PROBLEMS

1. Solve for x: $5/60 = x/600$. Then, $x = 50$

2. $960 \div 8 = 120$ days. Then, $120 - 60 = 60$ days

3. Storage area is $(175)(140) - (35)(75) - (10)(21) = 21,665$ sq.ft.

4. $9 \times 9 = 81$ sq.in. $(81)(10) = 810$ sq.in. of tiles cost $3.50. $(15ft)(21ft) = (180)(252) = 45,360$ sq.in. Now, $45,360 \div 810 = 56$ boxes. Finally, $(56)(\$3.50) = \$196$

5. $(2ft)(4ft)(4ft) = (24 in)(48 in)(48 in) = 55,296$ sq.in. Then, $55,296/27 = 2048$ boxes.

6. Balance at end of April 13th is $75 + 50 - 75 = 50$
   Balance at end of April 14th is $50 + 0 - 10 = 40$
   Balance at end of April 15th is $40 + 25 - 0 = 65$

7. $(4\ 1/2)(5) = 224$ sq.ft. Then, $(22)(\$0.10) = \$2.25$ per piece. The cost of 12 pieces is $(\$2.25)(12) = \$27$

8. If 10 man-hours are needed for 4 tons, then 200 man-hours are needed for 80 tons. The number of men needed to do the job in 20 hours is $200 \div 20 = 10$

9. 7 hours = 420 minutes and $420 \div 10 = 42$.
   Then, $(42)(12) = 504$ reams transported per day for each laborer. Now, $5000 \div 504 \approx 9.92$, which gets rounded up to 10.

10. $(9)(72) = 648$ package. Then, $\$64.80 \div 648 = \$0.10$

ARITHMETICAL REASONING
EXAMINATION SECTION
TEST 1

DIRECTIONS: Each question or incomplete statement is followed by several suggested answers or completions. Select the one that BEST answers the question or completes the statement. PRINT THE LETTER OF THE CORRECT ANSWER IN THE SPACE AT THE RIGHT.

1. When a certain gasoline tank is filled to capacity, it holds 420 gallons. If it is 3/4 full, the number of gallons of gasoline it is holding is   1.____

    A. 280   B. 315   C. 360   D. 375

2. Eight men working full time take 16 days to do a job. How long should it have taken if four men did this job?   2.____

    A. 26 Days   B. 28 Days   C. 32 Days   D. 38 Days

3. If 20 feet of lumber costs $ 62.00, the cost of 45 feet would be   3.____

    A. $136.25   B. $139.50   C. $144.25   D. $149.50

4. Shown below is a rectangle (JKLM) inside another rectangle (NPSR). What is the area of the shaded portion if LM measures 20 feet, JL measures 30 feet, NR measures 45 feet, and RS measures 55 feet?   4.____

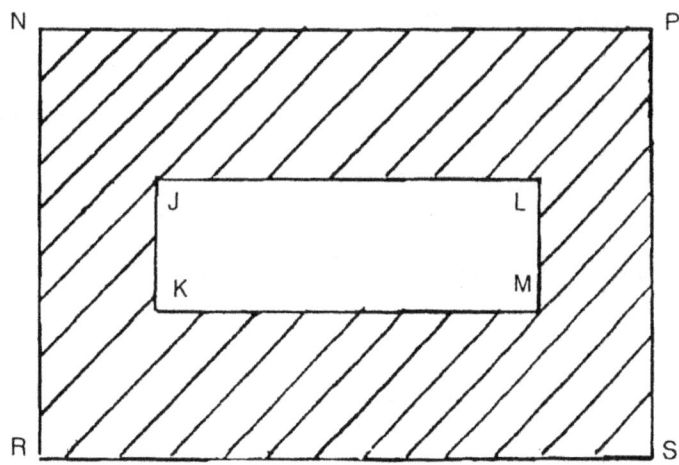

    A. 600 sq. ft.   B. 975 sq. ft.
    C. 1,875 sq. ft.   D. 2,475 sq. ft.

5. To produce a certain cleaning compound, four materials, W, X, Y, and Z, are combined by mixing 6 pounds of W, 5 pounds of X, 3 pounds of Y, and 1 pound of Z. In order to make up 270 pounds of this cleaning compound, the number of pounds of W required is _____ pounds.   5.____

    A. 100   B. 108   C. 112   D. 120

6. The normal work week for a laborer is 35 hours. If a laborer spends 27 hours at Job Location A and the rest of his work week at Job Location B, the percentage of time spent at Job Location B is, most nearly, _____ percent.

   A. 19	B. 21	C. 23	D. 25

7. If a 12-foot portable ladder meets the side of a building 11.625 feet from the ground, the distance from the base of the ladder to the side of the building should be, most nearly, _____ feet.

   A. 2	B. 3	C. 4	D. 6

8. A foreman must supply sufficient plywood paneling, each panel measuring 4 feet by 8 feet, to erect a three-sided barrier fence 8-feet-high in front of a building entrance. This rectangular area will be closed to the public while the building alterations are made. The longer side of the area measures 24 feet, and each of the shorter sides measures 12 feet. The *minimum* number of plywood panels necessary to erect this fence is

   A. 9	B. 12	C. 18	D. 24

9. An administrative assistant can process a certain type of report in 25 minutes. How many such reports could he *finish* processing in a workday from 9:00 a.m. to 5:00 p.m., with a 45-minute lunch break and two 10-minute coffee breaks?

   A. 16	B. 17	C. 18	D. 19

10. The income of a tenant family is as follows: the husband has a gross income of $140 per week; the wife has a gross income of $110 per week. Deductions from gross family income total $58 per week plus an allowable child-care expense of $28 per week. What is the *net* annual income of the family after deductions and allowable child-care expenses?

    A. $8,328	B. $8,528	C. $9,328	D. $9,528

KEY (CORRECT ANSWERS)

1. B
2. C
3. B
4. C
5. B

6. C
7. B
8. B
9. A
10. B

SOLUTIONS TO PROBLEMS

1. $(420)(3/4) = 315$ gallons

2. $(8)(16) = 128$ man-days. Then, $128 \div 4 = 32$ days.

3. $\$62 \div 20 = \$3.10$. Then, $(\$3.10)(45) = \$139.50$

4. Area of shaded portion is $(55)(45) - (30)(20) = 1875$ sq.ft.

5. The ratio of W to the entire compound is $6:15$ or $2:5 = \frac{2}{5}$.

   Then, $(270)(\frac{2}{5}) = 108$ pounds of W

6. $35 - 27 = 8$. Then, $8 \div 35 \approx .229$ or about 23%.

7. Let x = required distance. Then, $x^2 + (11.625)^2 = 12^2$ Simplifying, $x^2 + 135.14 = 144$. Then, $x^2 = 8.86$. So, $X \approx 3$ ft.

8. Number of panels needed for the long side is $24 \div 4 = 6$. Number of panels needed for each of two shorter sides is $12 \div 4 = 3$, Total number of panels is $6 + 3 + 3 = 12$.

9. 9:00 A.M. to 5:00 P.M. = 480 minutes.
   $480 - 45 - 10 - 10 = 415$ minutes of actual work.
   Then, $415 \div 25 = 16.6$, so that only 16 reports are <u>completely</u> finished.

10. $\$140 + \$110 - \$58 - \$28 = \$164$ per week.
    Then, $(\$164)(52) = \$8528$ per year.

TEST 2

Questions 1-2.

DIRECTIONS: Answer Questions 1 and 2 SOLELY on the basis of the following paragraph.

A housing development has 450 apartments. The average monthly rent is $134.50 per apartment. The average amount of subsidy money added to the average monthly rent (to meet the total operating costs) is $68.00. Since the time when the amount of the subsidy was determined, operating costs for the development have increased by $3960.00 per month.

1. If the subsidy is increased by 6%, what increase in the average monthly rental will be necessary to meet monthly operating costs?

    A. $3.40   B. $4.72   C. $8.80   D. No increase

2. What is the *new* total monthly operating cost per apartment?

    A. $76.80   B. $143.30   C. $211.30   D. $242.10

3. In a certain housing project, the average income of tenant families is $9,200 per annum and the average rent per apartment is $180 per month.
    If the average income increases 12% in a year while the average rent of an apartment increases 15%, how much more money will the average family have in a year after paying rent?

    A. $338.80   B. $780.00   C. $1120.80   D. $2484.00

4. A certain housing project has 1860 tenant families. It has two playgrounds, both rectangular in shape. One measures 104 feet by 45 feet; the other is 74 feet by 53 feet. The *number* of square feet of playground space per family in this project is, most nearly,

    A. 3   B. 5   C. 7   D. 9

5. A particular housing project has 1460 occupied apartments. If there are 12 new tenants in January, 14 in February, and 16 in March, the *turnover* rate for the first quarter of the year is, most nearly,

    A. 2.9%   B. 3.2%   C. 3.5%   D. 3.8%

Questions 6-7.

DIRECTIONS: Answer Questions 6 and 7 SOLELY on the basis of the following paragraph.

A tenant in a housing development receives a semi-monthly public assistance check of $117 and pays a monthly rental of $71 from the proceeds. The tenant is about to begin paying $9 additional per month toward total rent arrears of $136. At the same time that the arrears payments begin, his semi-monthly check increases to $121.

6. What will be the *total change* in monthly net income after all rent payments?

    A. $3   B. $2   C. $1   D. No change

7. If, instead of paying only $9 per month toward the arrears, the total increase in public assistance payments is used to increase arrears payments, how many months will it take the tenant to pay off the arrears?

   A. 8   B. 10   C. 12   D. 14

7._____

8. A tenant is offered two options in renewing a lease: (1) a one-year lease at a 10% increase in rent, or (2) a three-year lease at an 18% increase in rent. The tenant's current rent is $220.00 monthly.
   If the tenant takes the first option and continues to live in the apartment for three years with a 10% increase in rent each year, what would be the *difference* between the total rent he would pay and the rent he would have paid had he chosen the three-year lease?

   A. $266.64   B. $276.64   C. $1,425.60   D. $1,692.24

8._____

9. A certain task that an assistant performs takes approximately 45 minutes per unit of work. Seventy-five percent of his work-day is spent on this task.
   Assuming that he works seven hours per day, how many workdays will it take him to finish 1,470 units of work?

   A. 153   B. 210   C. 240   D. 270

9._____

10. It takes 5 1/2 gallons of paint to paint an average apartment, and it requires 18 man-hours.
    If the price of paint increases 24 cents per gallon and the pay of the painters increases 26.5 cents per hour, what is the *increase* in the cost of painting an apartment?

    A. $4.99   B. $5.09   C. $5.99   D. $6.09

10._____

KEY (CORRECT ANSWERS)

1. B
2. C
3. B
4. B
5. A

6. C
7. A
8. A
9. B
10. D

SOLUTIONS TO PROBLEMS

1. The increase per month in operating costs will be $3960 \div 450 = \$8.80$ per apartment. If the subside of \$68 is increased by 6%, this will amount to $(.06)(\$68) = \$4.08$ (per apartment). Thus, the necessary increase in the average monthly rental is $\$8.80 - \$4.08 = \$4.72$.

2. New total monthly operating cost per apartment is $\$134.50 + \$68 + (\$3960/450) = \$211.30$.

3. $\$9200 - (\$180)(12) = \$7040$. New income $= (\$9200)(1.12) = \$10,304$ per year. New annual rent $= (\$180)(12)(1.15) = \$2484$. Amount left over is $\$10,304 - \$2484 = \$7820$. Finally, $\$7820 - \$7040 = \$780$.

4. $(104)(45) + (74)(53) = 8602$ sq.ft.
   Then, $8602 \div 1860 \approx 4.62 = 5$ sq.ft. per family.

5. $(12 + 14 + 16) \div 1460 \approx .0288 \approx 2.9\%$

6. $[(\$117)(2) - \$71] - [(\$121)(2) - \$80] = \$1$

7. The monthly increase in public assistance payments is $(\$121 - \$117)(2) = \$8$. Now, the tenant is paying $\$8 + \$9 = \$17$ toward rent arrears. The number of months required is $\$136\ \$17 = 8$.

8. Choosing option 2, total rent paid after 3 years is $(\$220)(12)(3)(1.18) = \$9345,60$. With option 1, his rent for the 3 years will be $(\$220)(12)(1.10) + (\$220)(12)(1.10)^2 + (\$220)(12)(1.10)^3 = \$9612.24$. Finally, the savings by using option 2 is $\$9612.24 - \$9345.60 = \$266.64$.

9. $(.75)(7\text{ hours}) = 5.25$ hours $= 315$ minutes. Now, $315 \div 45 = 7$ units completed each day. Finally, $1470 \div 7 = 210$ days.

10. The increase is $(\$0.24)(5.5) + (\$0.265)(18) = \$6.09$.

TEST 3

DIRECTIONS: Each question or incomplete statement is followed by several suggested answers or completions. Select the one that BEST answers the question or completes the statement. PRINT THE LETTER OF THE CORRECT ANSWER IN THE SPACE AT THE RIGHT.

1. A foreman is directed to find out the percentage of contact rail insulators that should be replaced in one of his areas.
   The area has 2 tracks which are 660' long. The contact rails are 33' long. There are 4 insulators to a contact rail.
   There is a total of 16 insulators that should be replaced. The *percentage* of insulators that should be replaced is

   A. 10%   B. 15%   C. 20%   D. 25%

   1.____

2. If the scale on a detail drawing is 15/32" = 2', a scaled measurement of 4 7/32" represents an *actual* length of

   A. 14'   B. 16'   C. 18'   D. 20'

   2.____

3. A certain job takes 8 men a total of 8 days to complete if they work 2 hours of overtime each day.
   How long should this identical job take if it is done by 4 men without any overtime? (Assume that the actual number of hours a man works in a day without overtime is 8 hours, and assume that all of the men work at the same rate of speed.)

   A. 18 days   B. 19 days   C. 20 days   D. 21 days

   3.____

Questions 4-6.

DIRECTIONS: Questions 4 to 6 inclusive are based on the information given below.

A crew of 6 painters is going to paint only the walls of 75 rooms. The rooms have the following dimensions: 50 rooms are 35 feet long, 20 feet wide, with walls 10 feet high, and 25 rooms are 25 feet long, 15 feet wide, with walls 10 feet high. The walls are to be given two coats. The paint coverage is 400 square feet per gallon per coat. Assume a painter can cover 650 square feet of wall per 7-hour day. Assume that wall surfaces have windows and doors which constitute 10% of the wall surfaces and are not to be painted.

4. The *total* wall surface to be painted per coat of paint is, most nearly, _____ sq. ft.

   A. 65,300   B. 67,500   C. 69,500   D. 71,100

   4.____

5. Assume that the total wall surface to be painted is 75,000 square feet.
   The *total* number of gallons of paint needed for a complete job, neglecting any waste, is, most nearly,

   A. 358   B. 364   C. 370   D. 375

   5.____

6. The *total* number of working days required for the crew to cover 75,000 square feet of wall surface with 2 coats of paint is, most nearly, _____ days.

   A. 37   B. 39   C. 41   D. 43

   6.____

KEY (CORRECT ANSWERS)

1. A
2. C
3. C
4. B
5. D
6. B

SOLUTIONS TO PROBLEMS

1. Since there are 4 insulators for every 33 ft., and the sum of the two tanks is 1320 ft., the total number of insulators is (4)(1320/33) = 160. Finally, 16 ÷ 160 = 10%.

2. $4\frac{7}{32}" \div \frac{15}{32}" = 9$. Then, (9)(2') = 18'

3. The job requires (8)(8)(10) = 640 hours. Now, 4 men working 8 hours each day consume 32 hours. The number of days required is 640 ÷ 32 = 20.

4. Total wall surface area, in sq.ft., is [(10)(35)(2) + (10)(20)(2)] [50] + [(10)(25)(2) + (10)(15)(2)][25] - 10% of this number = (75,000)(.90) = 67,500.

5. 2 coats of paint means 150,000 sq.ft. of paint (75,000 given x 2).
   Then, 150,000 ÷ 400 = 375.

6. (75,000)(2) = 150,000 sq.ft. of paint. Each day, the amount of sq.ft. painted by all 6 painters is (6)(650) = 3900. Finally, 150,000 ÷ 3900 38.46 or most nearly 39 days.

ARITHMETICAL REASONING
EXAMINATION SECTION
TEST 1

DIRECTIONS: Briefly and concisely, solve each of the following problems, using the processes of arithmetic ONLY.

1. It is believed that every even number is the sum of two prime numbers. Two prime numbers whose sum is 32 are

    A. 7, 25   B. 11, 21   C. 13, 19   D. 17, 15

    1._____

2. To divide a number by 3000, we should move the decimal point 3 places to the _____ by 3.

    A. right and divide   B. left and divide
    C. right and multiply   D. left and multiply

    2._____

3. The difference between the area of a rectangle 6 ft. by 4 ft. and the area of a square having the same perimeter is

    A. 1 sq. ft.   B. 2 sq. ft.
    C. 4 sq. ft.   D. none of the above

    3._____

4. The ratio of 1/4 to 3/8 is the same as the ratio of

    A. 1 to 3   B. 2 to 3   C. 3 to 2   D. 3 to 4

    4._____

5. If 7 1/2 is divided by 1 1/5, the quotient is

    A. 6 1/4   B. 9   C. 7 1/10   D. 6 3/5

    5._____

6. A farmer has a cylindrical metal tank for watering his stock. It is 10 ft. in diameter and 3 ft. deep.
   If one cubic foot contains about 7.5 gallons, the APPROXIMATE capacity of the tank, in gallons, is

    A. 12   B. 225   C. 4   D. 1707

    6._____

7. The fraction which fits in the following series, 1/2, 1/10, _____ , 1/250 is

    A. 1/20   B. 1/100   C. 1/10   D. 1/50

    7._____

8. In two years $200 with interest compounded semi-annually at 4% will amount to

    A. $216.48   B. $233.92   C. $208   D. $216

    8._____

9. With a tax rate of .0200, a tax bill of $1050 corresponds to an assessed valuation of

    A. $21,000   B. $52,500   C. $21   D. $1029

    9._____

10. A sales agent, after deducting his commission of 6%, remits $2491 to his principal. The sale amounted to

    A. $2809   B. $2640   C. $2650   D. $2341.54

    10._____

11. The percent equivalent of .0295 is

    A. 2.95%   B. 29.5%   C. .295%   D. 295%

12. An angle of 105° is a(n) _____ angle.

    A. straight   B. acute   C. obtuse   D. reflex

13. A quart is approximately sixty cubic inches. A cubic foot of water weighs approximately sixty pounds.
    Therefore, a quart of water weighs APPROXIMATELY _____ lbs.

    A. 2   B. 3   C. 4   D. 5

14. If the same number is added to both the numerator and the denominator of a proper fraction, the

    A. value of the fraction is decreased
    B. value of the fraction is increased
    C. value of the fraction is unchanged
    D. effect of the operation depends on the original fraction

15. The LEAST common multiple of 3, 8, 9, 12 is

    A. 36   B. 72   C. 108   D. 144

16. On a bill of $100, the difference between a discount of 30% and 20% and a discount of 40% and 10% is

    A. nothing   B. $2   C. $20   D. 20%

17. 1/3 percent of a number is 24.
    The number is

    A. 8   B. 72   C. 800   D. 7200

18. The cost of importing five dozen china dinner sets, billed at $32 per set and paying a duty of 40%, is

    A. $224   B. $2688   C. $768   D. $1344

19. The net price of a television set is $756.
    If bought with a trade discount of 20%, and 10% for cash, the list price is

    A. $925.00   B. $957.80   C. $982.80   D. $1050.00

20. If Bob can complete a job in 6 hours and Steven can finish it in 8 hours, together they can complete the job in _____ hrs. _____ min.

    A. 2; 45   B. 3; 10   C. 3; 25   D. 4; 5

21. If the diameter is 80', the APPROXIMATE area of a skating rink is _____ square feet.

    A. 251.33   B. 1281.74   C. 2538.77   D. 5026.56

22. If an employer is subject to the Unemployment Insurance Fund and his quarterly payroll totals to $18,000, the quarterly tax payable to the Fund would be _____ (assuming the tax to be 2.7%).

    A. $233   B. $486   C. $977   D. $1,944

23. During a certain year, the weekly pay of John Smith was $900, his withholding tax 15%, and his Social Security tax was 4.4%.
    Then, Mr. Smith's take-home pay amounted to

    A. $685.85   B. $711.00   C. $725.40   D. $755.65

24. A 5% mortgage of $90,000 is for sale.
    What will the buyer have to pay for it to net 9%?

    A. $50,000   B. $85,500   C. $65,000   D. $81,900

25. If the passenger rate is $54, the operating cost per passenger to the railroad on the basis of 12 1/2% profit on fares is

    A. $6.75   B. $38.95   C. $47.25   D. $49.68

26. What is the amount of premium refunded to the insured if the insurance company cancels a 3-year policy at the end of 15 months?
    The rate is $30 per year.

    A. $37.50   B. $41.50   C. $43.00   D. $43.75

27. Suits originally selling for $200 were marked down to yield 20% on cost.
    If the original profit was 33 1/3% on cost, the new sales price will be

    A. $134   B. $160   C. $171   D. $180

28. If he works 10 hours on Tuesday and 12 hours on Friday, and regular hours on the other days, for an 8-hour day, 5 days per week, daily pay $120, Samuels will earn _____ (time and a half for overtime).

    A. $600   B. $735   C. $750   D. $785

29. To provide 10,000 typewriting sheets (8 1/2 x 11), the mill will have to cut how many reams of folio stock which measures 17 x 22?

    A. 5   B. 6 1/2   C. 8   D. 10

30. Property worth $1.6 million was insured for $1 million under a policy containing the 80% co-insurance clause. The damage amounted to $960,000.
    The insured will collect

    A. $480,000   B. $650,000   C. $750,000   D. $780,000

31. At the rate of $1.68 for the Sterling, what will the traveler require in American currency to meet expenses and purchases of goods calling for £20 6s. 6d?

    A. $21.34   B. $34.15   C. $38.21   D. $57.12

32. The proceeds of a 6% interest-bearing note for $800 due in 45 days and discounted 15 days after it was dated, at the rate of 5%, will be

    A. $796.25   B. $802.64   C. $804.93   D. $805.92

33. $4.80 is .08% of

    A. $600   B. $6000   C. $6500   D. $60,000

34. If 25% of a classroom register consists of boys, the ratio of girls to boys is

    A. 4:1   B. 3:1   C. 1:4   D. 1:3

35. If a wage earner who is over 65 years of age, married (wife's age 55) and 2 other dependents whose earnings are below $2,300, pays his Federal income tax, what will his TOTAL exemptions add up to?

    A. 2   B. 3   C. 4   D. 5

36. An equality of ratios is another term for

    A. proportion   B. equilibrium
    C. summation   D. inversion

37. A kilometer is APPROXIMATELY what part of a mile?

    A. 0.059   B. 0.062   C. 0.064   D. 0.067

38. Two liters is a _____ quantity than two quarts.

    A. smaller dry quart/larger liquid quart
    B. larger dry quart/smaller liquid quart
    C. smaller dry quart/smaller liquid quart
    D. larger dry quart/larger liquid quart

39. The square root of 46.24 is

    A. 6.793   B. 6.800   C. 7.984   D. 9.248

40. Ordinary interest is _____ than exact interest for the same time and at the same rate.

    A. less   B. more   C. equal   D. variable

41. After all taxes have been added on, what will the coat cost the purchaser if the advertised price of a natural mink coat is $8,000? (Assume Federal Sales Tax is 10% and the Local Sales Tax is 8 1/4%.)

    A. $8660   B. $9460   C. $9526   D. $9548

42. A ring bearing the mark 12K on the inside contains _____ parts gold and 12 parts alloy.

    A. 2   B. 12   C. 6   D. 14

43. The sounding line recorded a depth of 20 fathoms or _____ feet.

    A. 110   B. 120   C. 130   D. 140

44. If a pound of green peanuts costs $1.25 and peanuts lose 1/6 of its weight in the roasting process, what is the cost of the roasted peanuts?

    A. $1.00   B. $1.20   C. $1.25   D. $1.50

45. A cubic foot (liquid measure) is APPROXIMATELY how many gallons?

    A. 7.48   B. 7.55   C. 7.65   D. 7.80

46. If the closing price of USX Corp. reads 76 1/2 followed by -1/4, it indicates that the previous day's closing price was   46.____

    A. 76 3/4   B. 76 1/2   C. 76 5/8   D. 76 3/8

47. An inscription on the cornerstone of a building reads MDCXCIV. This means that the cornerstone was placed there in the year   47.____

    A. 1484   B. 1594   C. 1694   D. 1794

48. 12 plus 6 x 6 less 24 ÷ 6 plus 10 equals   48.____

    A. 44   B. 64   C. 54   D. 14

49. A motorist travels 120 miles to his destination at the average speed of 60 miles per hour and returns to the starting point at the average speed of 40 miles per hour. His AVERAGE speed for the entire trip is _____ miles per hour.   49.____

    A. 53   B. 50   C. 48   D. 45

50. A snapshot measures 2 1/2 inches by 1 7/8 inches. It is to be enlarged so that the longer dimension will be 4 inches. The length of the enlarged shorter dimension will be _____ inches.   50.____

    A. 2 1/2   B. 3 3/8
    C. 3   D. none of the above

KEY (CORRECT ANSWERS)

1. C	11. A	21. D	31. B	41. B
2. B	12. C	22. D	32. B	42. B
3. A	13. A	23. C	33. B	43. B
4. B	14. B	24. A	34. B	44. D
5. A	15. B	25. C	35. C	45. A
6. B	16. B	26. D	36. A	46. A
7. D	17. D	27. D	37. B	47. C
8. A	18. B	28. B	38. A	48. C
9. B	19. D	29. A	39. B	49. C
10. C	20. C	30. C	40. B	50. C

SOLUTIONS TO PROBLEMS

1. CORRECT ANSWER: C
   A prime number is an integer which cannot be divided except by itself and one integer; a whole number as opposed to a fraction or a decimal.

2. CORRECT ANSWER: B

   $$3\overline{)6.000}\begin{array}{c}2\end{array}$$ Example: Divide 6000 by 3000

3. CORRECT ANSWER: A

    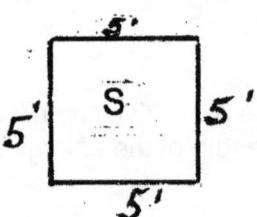

   P = 20 ft.   P = 20 ft.
   A = 24 sq. ft.   A = 25 sq. ft.

   $$\begin{array}{r}25\\-24\\\hline 1\end{array}$$

4. CORRECT ANSWER: B

   $$\frac{1/4}{3/8} = 1/4 \div 3/8 = 1/4 \times 8/3 = 2/3$$

5. CORRECT ANSWER: A

   $$\frac{7\frac{1}{2}}{1\,1/5} = \frac{15}{2} \div \frac{6}{5} = \frac{15}{2} \times \frac{5}{6} = \frac{25}{4} = 6\frac{1}{4}$$

   OR

   $$1.2\overline{)7.5}\begin{array}{c}6\frac{\cancel{3}}{\cancel{12}}\frac{1}{4}\end{array}$$

6. CORRECT ANSWER: B

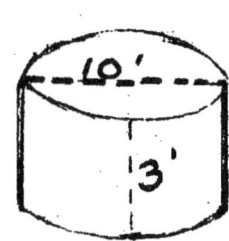

$A = \pi R^2$
$= 3(5)^2$
$= 75$ sq. ft.

$\pi = \dfrac{22}{7} = 3$ (approx.)

Volume of tank $= 75 \times 3 = 225$ cu. ft.
(approximate capacity of tank in gallons)

```
   225
  x7.5
  ----
  1125
  1575
  ------
  1687.5 gal.
```

7. CORRECT ANSWER: D
A geometric series: each number is multiplied by the same number to get the succeeding number. (Multiply each number by 1/5.)

1/2, 1/10, 1/50, 1/250

8. CORRECT ANSWER: A
<u>Compound Interest</u>
4% a year compounded semi-annually is the same as 2% for a half year.

(a) $200
    x .02

    $4.00 Interest for 1st half year

    $200
    + 4

    $204 Principal for 1st half year

(b) $204
    x .02

    $4.08 Interest for 2nd half year

    $204.00
    + 4.08

    $208.08 Principal for 1st half
            of 2nd year

(c) $208.08
    x   .02

    $4.1616 Interest for 1st half
            of 2nd year

    $208.08
    + 4.16

    $212.24 Principal for 2nd
            half of 2nd year

(d) $212.24
    x   .02

    $4.2448 Interest for 2nd half
            of 2nd year

    $212.24
    + 4.24

    $216.48 Principal at end of
            2nd half of 2nd year

9. CORRECT ANSWER: B
    .0200x = $1050
     200x = $10,500,000
       2x = $105,000
        x = $52,500 (assessed valuation)

10. CORRECT ANSWER: C

$2491 + .06x = x   Proof
x = 2491 + .06x $2650 $2491
1.00x - .06x = 2491   × .06   + 159
.94x = 2491 $159.00 $2650
94x = 249,100

$$94\overline{)249{,}100} = \$2{,}650$$

11. CORRECT ANSWER: A
.0295 = 2.95%

12. CORRECT ANSWER: C
An obtuse angle is an angle greater than 90°.

13. CORRECT ANSWER: A
A quart = 60 cu. in.
80 lbs. = 1 cu. ft. (or 1728 cu.in.)(12x12x12)
           (Keep like units of measure together)
60 lbs. = 1728 cu.in.

1 lb. = $\dfrac{1728}{60}$ = approximately .29 cu. in.

If 29 cu.in. weigh 1 lb., then 60 cu.in. weighs 2 lbs. (approx). Therefore, a quart weighs 2 lbs. (approx.).

14. CORRECT ANSWER: B
(1) Start with the fraction 2/3

(2) $\dfrac{2+2}{3+2} = \dfrac{4}{5}$ (Adding 2 to the numerator and the denominator)

(3) $\dfrac{2}{3} = \dfrac{10}{15}$

(4) $\dfrac{4}{5} = \dfrac{12}{15}$

15. CORRECT ANSWER: B
Common multiple: can be evenly divided by all the numbers. Least common multiple: the lowest of these numbers (72).

16. CORRECT ANSWER: B
Formula
    Step 1. Express percentages as decimals
    Step 2. Subtract each discount from one
    Step 3. Multiply all the results
    Step 4. Subtract the product from one

    Step 1. .3, .2, and .4, .1

Step 2. .7, .8, and .6, .9
Step 3. .7 x .8 = .56 (represents percent remaining after the .6 x .9 = .54 discounts are taken)
Step 4.
```
 1.00       1.00
 -.56       -.54
  .44        .46
```
The difference is 2%
Then, $100 x .02 = $2.00.

17. CORRECT ANSWER: D

$\frac{1}{300} x = 24$

x = 24 x 300
x = 7200

18. CORRECT ANSWER: B

```
   $32
 x  60
 $1920
```
(Cost of dinner sets before paying duty)

```
 $1920
 x  .40
 $768.00
```
(Duty)

```
 $1920
 + 768
 $2688
```

19. CORRECT ANSWER: D

Single discount for 20% and 10% = 28%

```
 20 + 10    = 30
 20 x 10%   =  2.0
              28.0
```

List Price - Discount = Net Price
100% - 28% = 72%
$756 = 72% of List Price

```
        1050
 72)$75600
     72
     360
     360
```

20. CORRECT ANSWER: C

$\frac{1}{6} + \frac{1}{8} = \frac{7}{24}$ (job done in 1 hour by both)

$\therefore 24 \div 7 = 3\frac{3}{7}$ (hours together)

= 3 hours, 25 minutes

21. CORRECT ANSWER: D

Area = πr^2

= $3.1416 \times (40')^2 = 3.1416 \times 1600 = 5026.56$ sq. ft.

22. CORRECT ANSWER: B

18,000 x 2.7% = $486 (quarterly) or $1,944 (annually)

23. CORRECT ANSWER: C

1) $900 x 15% = $135 (Withholding Tax)
2) $900 x 4.4% = $39.60 (Social Security Tax)
$174.60 (Total Tax Deduction)
$900 - $174.60 = $725.40 (Take-home Pay)

24. CORRECT ANSWER: A

5% of $90,000 = $4,500 (income for one year)
To obtain 9%, the cost of the mortgage must be:

$4,500 = \frac{9}{100}$ of the mortgage

$4,500 \times \frac{100}{9} = \$50,000$ (cost of mortgage)

25. CORRECT ANSWER: C

Passenger rate = $54
Profit = 6.75 (1/8 of 54)
Operating Cost = $47.25

26. CORRECT ANSWER: D

30 x 2 1/2 = $75 (premium for 3 years)
36 months - 15 months = 21 months unexpired time

$\frac{21}{36} \times 75 = \$43.75$ (amount to be refunded)

27. CORRECT ANSWER: D

L.P. = $200 = 133 1/3% of cost
Cost = 100%
Profit = 33 1/3%

11 (#1)

```
        200 =       1 1/3 of the cost
   200 x 3/4 =      $150 cost
   $150 x 1/5 =     $30 new profit
   $150 + $30 =     $180 new marked price
```

28. CORRECT ANSWER: B

	Regular Time	Overtime
Monday	8	
Tuesday	8	2
Wednesday	8	
Thursday	8	
Friday	8	4
	40 hours	6 hours

Rate per hour = $120 / 8 hours = $15 per hour
Overtime = 6 hours x 1 1/2 x $15 = $22.50 overtime pay x 6 hrs. = $135
Payment for regular time worked = 40 hours x $15 = $600
Samuels earned $135 + $600 = $735

29. CORRECT ANSWER: A
500 sheets = 1 ream of paper
1 ream 17x22 = 4 sheets 8 1/2 x 11
500 sheets x 4 = 2000 sheets from 1 ream (17x22)
∴ 10,000 sheets may be obtained from 5 reams (17x22)

30. CORRECT ANSWER: C

$$\frac{1 \text{ million}}{4/5 \times 1.6 \text{ mil.}} \times 960,000 = \$750,000$$

31. CORRECT ANSWER: B (12 pence (d) = 1 shilling(s);

```
   6s  = .3£            20 s = 1 pound (£);
   .5s = .025£           6d  = .5s)
         .325£
```

∴ $1.68 x 20.325 = $34.15

32. CORRECT ANSWER: B
Maturation value of $800 note at 6% interest for 45 days may be computed as follows:
   $800 + (1/8 x .06 x 800) = 800 + 6 = $806 (maturation value)

```
Interest is $8.06 for  72  days  at  5%
Interest is $4.03 for  36  days  at  5%
Interest is    .67 for   6  days  at  5%
Interest is $3.36 for  30  days  at  5%
Finally, maturation value = $806.00
             discount    =    3.36
             proceeds    = $802.64
```

33. **CORRECT ANSWER: B**
    $4.80 ÷ .0008 = $6000

34. **CORRECT ANSWER: B**
    Boys = 1/4 of class
    ∴ Girls = 3/4 of class
    Ratio is 3 to 1 (girls to boys)

35. **CORRECT ANSWER: C**
    Exemptions: 1 + 1 + 2 = 4

36. **CORRECT ANSWER: A**
    Proportion

37. **CORRECT ANSWER: B**
    39.37 inches = 1 meter
    3937 inches = 1 kilometer
    1 kilometer = 3937 ÷ 12 = 328.08 ft.
    ∴ 328.08 ÷ 5280 = .0621

38. **CORRECT ANSWER: A**
    1 liter = 0.9081 U.S. dry quart ANSWER: Smaller (U.S. dry quart)
    1 liter = 1.0567 U.S. liquid quarts ANSWER: Larger (U.S. liquid quart)

39. **CORRECT ANSWER: B**

    $$\begin{array}{r} 6.8 \\ 22\overline{)46.24} \\ 36 \\ 128\overline{)1024} \\ 1024 \end{array}$$

40. **CORRECT ANSWER: B**
    More

41. **CORRECT ANSWER: B**
    $8000 + $800 (Federal Tax 10%) + $660 (Local Sales Tax 3%) = $9460

42. **CORRECT ANSWER: B**
    Gold marked 12K is 12/24 pure and 12/24 alloy.

43. **CORRECT ANSWER: B**
    1 fathom = 6 feet

44. **CORRECT ANSWER: D**
    Cost = $1.25, which is 5/6 of the cost of the roasted peanuts
    ∴ $1.25 x 6/5 = $1.50, the cost of 1 lb. of roasted peanuts.

13 (#1)

45. CORRECT ANSWER: A
231 cu.in. = 1 gallon
1 cu.ft. = 12" x 12" x 12" = 1728 cu.in.
1728 ÷ 231 = 7.48 gallons

46. CORRECT ANSWER: A
76 1/2 + 1/4 = 76 3/4 (previous day's closing)

47. CORRECT ANSWER: C
M = 1000
DC = 600
XC =   90
IV =   4

      1694

48. CORRECT ANSWER: C
12 + 36 - 4 + 10 = 54
Order of Operations:
In order to find the value of a number expression:
1. First, do all the multiplications
2. Second, do the divisions, taking them in order from left to right
3. Finally, do the additions and subtractions, taking them in any order

49. CORRECT ANSWER: C
120 miles = 2 hours (60 mph)
120 miles = 3 hours (40 mph)
240 miles = 5 hours = average of 48 mph

50. CORRECT ANSWER: C
Change 2 1/2 to 20/8

Change 1 7/8 to 15/8
Ratio is 20 to 15 or 4 to 3
If the longer dimension is 4 inches, then the shorter is 3 inches.

EXAMINATION SECTION
TEST 1

DIRECTIONS: Each question or incomplete statement is followed by several suggested answers or completions. Select the one that BEST answers the question or completes the statement. *PRINT THE LETTER OF THE CORRECT ANSWER IN THE SPACE AT THE RIGHT.*

1. Butter is quoted at $ 2 a pound or 54 cents a quarter pound. The percent increase over the pound rate is

    A. 2 B. 4 C. 6 D. 8

2. A square has the same area as an oblong 16 inches long and 4 inches wide. The perimeter of the oblong

    A. exceeds the perimeter of the square by 100 percent
    B. equals the perimeter of the square
    C. is less than the perimeter of the square by 8 inches
    D. exceeds the perimeter of the square by 8 inches

3. A jet plane made the trip from Albany to New York, a distance of 150 miles, in 15 minutes. The speed of sound is approximately 700 miles per hour. This exceeds the speed of the plane, in miles per hour, by

    A. 50 B. 100 C. 150 D. 650

4. The scale on a certain map is given as 1 1/2 inches to 500 miles. The distance represented by 5 inches is approximately _____ miles.

    A. 1150 B. 1300 C. 1650 D. 3000

5. If money is invested at 4 percent compounded semi-annually, it will double in 17 1/2 years.
   If interest is compounded at the same rate annually, the number of years in which it will be doubled is

    A. 17 1/2
    B. more than 17 1/2
    C. less than 17 1/2
    D. not determinable without additional data

6. Given: 1 inch = 2.54 centimeters; the number of centimeters by which one meter exceeds one yard is approximately

    A. 3 B. 10 C. 15 D. 90

7. If a baseball team has won ten games and has lost five games, its standing is given by the fraction

    A. .667 B. .500 C. .339 D. .200

2 (#1)

8. Two persons start out driving from a given point, one driving north at the rate of thirty miles an hour, and the other driving east at the rate of forty miles an hour. At the end of two hours of continuous driving, they will have reached points the distance between which, in miles, is

   A. 140 B. 50 C. 100 D. 70

   8.____

9. Three-eighths of a percent of 1600 is

   A. 600 B. 60 C. 6 D. 0.6

   9.____

10. For which of the following is the answer 1/3 NOT correct?

    A. $18 \div ? = 54$ B. $16 \times ? = 5\ 2/3$
    C. $4 - ? = 3\ 2/3$ D. $? \div 2/3 = 1/2$

    10.____

11. A quart is approximately 60 cu. in. A cubic foot of water weighs approximately 60 lbs. Therefore, a quart of water weighs APPROXIMATELY _____ lbs.

    A. 2 B. 3 C. 4 D. 5

    11.____

12. A dealer purchases a gross of pads for $4.00 and sells all of them at the rate of three pads for 25 cents.
    His rate of profit, based on the cost, is

    A. 66 2/3¢ B. 150% C. 200% D. 300%

    12.____

13. In the simplest form, -11 - (-2) is

    A. 7 B. 9 C. -11 D. -9

    13.____

14. Find the average of 6.46, 5.89, 3.42, .65, 7.09.

    A. 5.812 B. 4.704 C. 3.920 D. 4.705

    14.____

15. $\dfrac{456.3}{0.89}$ equals

    A. 513.89 13/89   B. 512.69 59/89
    C. 513.89 59/89   D. 512.89 59/89

    15.____

16. Add 5 hrs. 13 min., 3 hrs. 49 min., and 14 min. The sum is _____ hrs. _____ mins.

    A. 9; 16 B. 8; 16 C. 9; 76 D. 8; 6

    16.____

17. Suits sold at $65 each. The suits cost $50 each.
    The percentage of increase of the selling price over the cost is

    A. 40% B. 33 1/3% C. 33 1/2% D. 30%

    17.____

18. Change 0.03125 to a common fraction.

    A. 3/64 B. 1/6 C. 1/64 D. 1/32

    18.____

19. Divide 7/8 by 7/8.

    A. 1 B. 0 C. 7/8 D. 49/64

    19.____

20. A worked 5 days on overhauling an old car. B worked 4 days more to finish the job. After the sale of the car, the net profit was $243. They wanted to divide the profit on the basis of the time spent by each.
    A's share of the profit was

    A. $108   B. $135   C. $127   D. $143

21. If A takes 6 days to do a task and B takes 3 days to do the same task, working together they should do the same task in _____ days.

    A. 2 2/3   B. 2   C. 2 1/3   D. 2 1/2

22. In the series 5, 8, 13, 20, the NEXT number should be

    A. 23   B. 26   C. 29   D. 32

23. The interest on $300 at 6% for 10 days is (use 6% method)

    A. $.50   B. $1.50   C. $2.50   D. $5.50

24. If the scale on a map indicates that 1 1/2 inches equals 500 miles, then 5 inches on that map will represent APPROXIMATELY _____ males.

    A. 1800   B. 1600   C. 1300   D. 700

25. 1/2% equals

    A. .002   B. .020   C. .005   D. .050

26. If an employee drew $260 which was 20% of his bonus, his entire bonus was

    A. $2300   B. $2600   C. $1600   D. $1300

27. If a kilogram equals about 35 ounces, the number of grams in one ounce is about

    A. 29   B. 30   C. 31   D. 32

28. The area of a mirror 40 inches long and 20 inches wide is APPROXIMATELY _____ square feet.

    A. 8.5   B. 5.5   C. 8.0   D. 5.0

29. The price per gross of items which sell at the rate of 20 for 30¢ is

    A. $2.16   B. $1.80   C. $3.60   D. $2.40

30. If sound travels at the rate of 1100 ft. per second, in one half minute it will travel about _____ miles.

    A. 6   B. 8   C. 10   D. 3

31. If a kilometer is about 5/8 of a mile, 2 miles are about _____ kilometers.

    A. 1.6   B. 3.2   C. 2.4   D. 75

32. A lecture hall which is 25 ft. wide and 75 ft. long has a perimeter equal to _____ feet(yards).

    A. 1750   B. 200   C. 66 2/3   D. 1875

33. After deducting a discount of 16 2/3%, the price of a coat was $35.00. The list price was

    A. $37.50   B. $38.00   C. $41.75   D. $42.00

34. The number which increased by 1/6 of itself results in 182 is

    A. 156   B. 176   C. 148   D. 160

35. 26,932.43 minus 18,345.86 is

    A. 8,568.75   B. 8,865.57   C. 8,856.75   D. 8,586.57

36. 19 2/3 diminished by 7 1/4 is

    A. 12 1/3   B. 12 3/4   C. 12 5/12   D. 12 1/4

37. 2/3 plus 7/8 plus 1/4 minus 5/9 equals

    A. 37/72   B. 89/72   C. 43/72   D. 55/72

38. The number of years between Caesar's death in 55 B.C. and the fall of Rome in 476 is

    A. 411   B. 531   C. 421   D. 481

39. 1/6 of 9 yards is _____ yards(feet).

    A. 1 2/3   B. 4 2/3   C. 4 1/2   D. 4 1/3

40. 33 1/3% is APPROXIMATELY

    A. 333.3   B. 33.33   C. 3.333   D. .3333

41. On a list price of $200, the difference between a single discount of 25% and successive discounts of 20% and 5% is

    A. $50   B. $48   C. $2   D. $0

42. If a man has only quarters and dimes totaling $2.00, the number of quarters CANNOT be

    A. 2   B. 4   C. 6   D. 3

43. The standing of a baseball team of the 7th grade which won ten games and lost five games is

    A. .667   B. .500   C. .333   D. .200

44. The number of cubic feet of soil needed for a flower box 3 ft. long, 8 in. wide, and 1 ft. deep is

    A. 24   B. 12   C. 4 2/3   D. 2

45. At $1250 per hundred, 288 watches will cost

    A. $3,600   B. $36,000   C. $2,880   D. $360

46. On February 12, 2014, the age of a boy who was born on March 15, 1994 will be _____ years, _____ months, _____ days.

    A. 20; 10; 3   B. 19; 9; 27   C. 20; 1; 3   D. 19; 10; 27

47. On February 12, 2019, the age of a teacher who was born on December 26, 1949 will be _____ years, _____ months, _____ days.   47.____

   A. 70; 2; 26
   B. 69; 1; 16
   C. 69; 10; 26
   D. 70; 2; 16

48. At a simple interest rate of 5% a year, the principal that will give $12.50 interest in 6 months is   48.____

   A. $250
   B. $500
   C. $625
   D. $650

49. If John must have a mark of 80% to pass a test of 35 items, the number of items he may miss and still pass the test is   49.____

   A. 7
   B. 8
   C. 11
   D. 28

50.   50.____

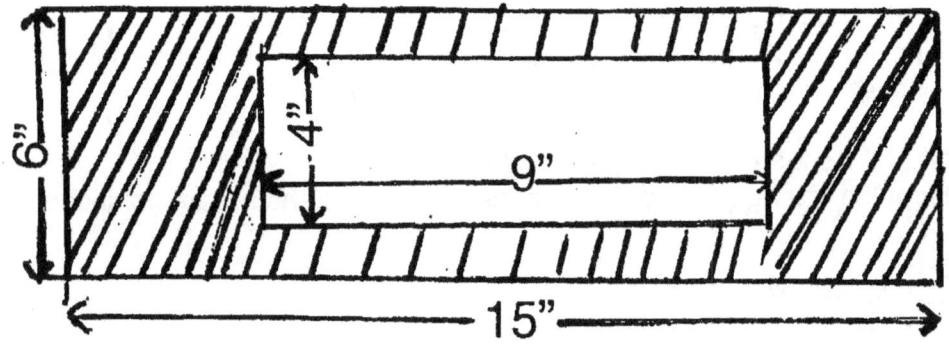

The area of the shaded portion of the above rectangle is _____ square inches.

   A. 54
   B. 90
   C. 45
   D. 36

KEY (CORRECT ANSWERS)

1. D	11. A	21. B	31. B	41. C
2. D	12. C	22. C	32. C	42. D
3. B	13. D	23. A	33. D	43. A
4. C	14. B	24. B	34. A	44. D
5. B	15. B	25. C	35. D	45. A
6. B	16. A	26. D	36. C	46. D
7. A	17. D	27. A	37. B	47. B
8. C	18. D	28. B	38. B	48. B
9. C	19. A	29. A	39. C	49. A
10. B	20. B	30. A	40. D	50. A

SOLUTIONS TO PROBLEMS

1. **CORRECT ANSWER: D**
   $.54 x 4 = $2.16
   (lb.rate) = 2.00
   Increase .16

   $$\frac{.16}{200} = \frac{8}{100} = 8\%$$

2. **CORRECT ANSWER: D**
   16 inches x 4 inches = 64 square inches
   Perimeter of the oblong is:

16 inches	x	2 inches	=	32 inches
4 inches	x	2 inches	=	8 inches
				40 inches

   Perimeter of the square is: 8 inches x 4 = 32 inches
   Perimeter of the oblong (40 inches) exceeds perimeter of the square (32 inches) by 8 inches.

3. **CORRECT ANSWER: B**
   150 miles in 15 minutes = 600 miles in 60 minutes (1 hour)
   700 - 600 = 100 mph excess of speed of sound over plane.

4. **CORRECT ANSWER: C**
   5 inches is 3 1/3 times as great as 1 1/2 inches.
   (3/2 is to 10/2) 500 x 3 1/3 = 1666 2/3 miles or 1650 approximately (closest)

5. **CORRECT ANSWER: B**
   The longer the period used to calculate compound interest, the smaller the interest amount. Answer must be over 17 1/2 years.

6. **CORRECT ANSWER: B**
   1 inch = 2.54 centimeters

   39.37 inches = 1 meter
   −36. inches = 1 yard
   _____
   3.37 inches = excess of one meter over one yard

   3.37 x 2.54 = 8.5598 centimeters
   Nearest answer is 10 centimeters.

7. **CORRECT ANSWER: A**
   The team has won 10 out of 15 or 10/15 = .667

8. **CORRECT ANSWER: C**
   $a^2 + b^2 = c^2$
   $60^2 + 80^2 = c^2$
   $3600 + 6400 = c^2$
   $10{,}000 = c^2$
   $c = \sqrt{10{,}000}$ or 100

9. **CORRECT ANSWER: C**
   1600 x .00375 = 6 or (1600 x 3/8) ÷ 100 = 6

10. **CORRECT ANSWER: B**
    18 ÷ 1/3 = 54
    16 x 1/3 = 5 1/3 (NOT 5 2/3)
    4 - 3 2/3 = 1/3
    1/3 ÷ 2/3 = 1/2

11. **CORRECT ANSWER: A**
    1728 cubic inches = 1 cubic foot
    1728:60 = 60:x
    1728 x = 3600
    $x = \dfrac{3600}{1728} = 2 +$ lbs.

12. **CORRECT ANSWER: C**
    144 ÷ 3 = 48 x .25 = $12.00 Selling Price
                                4.00 Cost
                              $ 8.00 Profit

    $\dfrac{8.00}{4.00} = \dfrac{2}{1} = 200\%$

13. **CORRECT ANSWER: D**
    -11 - (-2) = 11 + 2 = -9

14. **CORRECT ANSWER: B**
    6.47
    5.89
    3.42
     .65
    7.09   4.704
    23.520   5)23.520

15. **CORRECT ANSWER: B**

```
              5 12.69
    0.89.)456.30.00
         445
         ‾‾‾
          11 3
           8 9
          ‾‾‾
           2 40
           1 78
          ‾‾‾‾
             620
             534
            ‾‾‾
             860
             801
            ‾‾‾
              59
```

16. **CORRECT ANSWER: A**

   5' 13"
   3' 49"
       14"
   ‾‾‾‾‾‾
   9' 16"

17. **CORRECT ANSWER: D**
   Increase of the selling price over the cost = $15 ($65 - $50)

   $\therefore \dfrac{\$15}{\$30} = 30\%$ (percentage of increase of the selling price over the cost)

18. **CORRECT ANSWER: D**

   $0.03125 = \dfrac{03125}{100000} = \dfrac{1}{32}$

19. **CORRECT ANSWER: A**

   $\dfrac{\frac{7}{8}}{\frac{7}{8}} = \dfrac{7}{8} \times \dfrac{8}{1} = 1$

20. **CORRECT ANSWER: B**
    A = 5/9 of the work
    B = 4/9 of the work
    5/9 x 243 = 5 x 27 = $135

21. **CORRECT ANSWER: B**
    A does 1/6 of the task in one day
    B does 1/3 of the task in one day
    (adding) 1/6 + 1/3 = 3/6 = 1/2 of task in one day
    $\therefore$ It takes 2 days for A and B working together to do the same task.

22. **CORRECT ANSWER: C**
5, 8, 13, 20 .... This series progresses by adding 3, 5, 7, respectively, to each of the first three numbers above. Therefore, 9 should be added to the fourth number (20), making the next number in the series 29.

23. **CORRECT ANSWER: A**
$300 x .06 = $18.00
∴ $18.00 ÷ 1/36 (10 days = 1/36 of 360 days) = $.50

24. **CORRECT ANSWER: B**
$$\frac{5}{1\frac{1}{2}} = \frac{5}{\frac{3}{2}} = 5 \times \frac{2}{3} = \frac{10}{3} = 3\ 1/3$$
∴ 500 x 3 1/3 = 500 x 10/3 = 5000/3 = 1666 2/3

25. **CORRECT ANSWER: C**
1/2% = .005 (by inspection)

26. **CORRECT ANSWER: D**
If $260 = 1/5 (20%) of his bonus, then $260 x 5 = $1300 (his entire bonus)

27. **CORRECT ANSWER: A**
A kilogram = 1000 grams (by definition)
∴ $\frac{1000}{35}$ = 28.57⁺ (the number of grams in one ounce)

Work
```
       28.57
   35)1000.00
       70
       300
       280
       200
       175
       250
       245
```

28. **CORRECT ANSWER: B**
40" x 20" = 800 sq. in.
∴ 800 144 (there are 144 sq. in. in 1 sq. ft.) = 5.5⁺ sq. ft.

Work
```
        5.5
   144)800.0
       720
       80 0
       72 0
```

29. **CORRECT ANSWER: A**
30¢ ÷ 20 = 1 1/2¢ (price per 1 item)
∴ 144 x 1 1/2¢ = $2.16 (price per gross)

30. **CORRECT ANSWER: A**
1100 ft. per second = 33,000 ft. in 1/2 minute (30 x 1100) There are 5280 ft. in a mile.
∴ 33,000 ÷ 5280 = 6⁺ miles

31. **CORRECT ANSWER: B**
$$\frac{2}{\frac{5}{8}} = 2 \times \frac{8}{5} = \frac{16}{5} = \frac{31}{5} = 3.2$$

32. **CORRECT ANSWER: C**
Perimeter = the sum of the four sides
= 25+25+75+75
= 200 feet
= 66 2/3 yards

33. **CORRECT ANSWER: D**
16 2/3% = 1/6
$35.00 = 5/6 of the list price
$$\therefore \frac{35}{\frac{5}{6}} = 35 \times \frac{6}{5} = \$42.00$$

34. **CORRECT ANSWER: A**
Let x = the number
∴ 7/6x = 182
$$x = \frac{182}{\frac{7}{6}} = 182 \times 6/7 = 156$$

35. **CORRECT ANSWER: D**
```
  26,932.43
 -18,345.86
  ─────────
   8,586.57
```

36. **CORRECT ANSWER: C**

$$19 \tfrac{2}{3} \quad \tfrac{12}{8}$$
$$7 \tfrac{1}{4} \quad 3$$
$$1_2 \quad \tfrac{5}{12}$$

37. **CORRECT ANSWER: B**

11 (#1)

$$\begin{array}{r|l} & 24 \\ \frac{2}{3} & 16 \\ \frac{7}{8} & 21 \\ \frac{1}{4} & 6 \\ \hline & \frac{43}{24} \end{array}$$

(2) $\dfrac{43}{24} \cdot \dfrac{5}{9} =$

$\dfrac{129}{72} - \dfrac{40}{72} =$ (changing fractions to multiples of 72)

$\dfrac{89}{72}$

38. **CORRECT ANSWER: B**

    55
    +476
    531

39. **CORRECT ANSWER: C**
    9 yards = 27 feet
    We then simply take 1/6 of 27, viz.: 1/6 x 27 = 4 1/2 feet

40. **CORRECT ANSWER: D**
    33 1/3% = .3333 (by inspection)

41. **CORRECT ANSWER: C**
    Single discount of 25% - $200 x .25 = .$50
                                 200 - $50 = $150
    Successive discounts of 20% and 5%
    $200 x .20 = $40; $200 - $40 = $160
    $160 x .05 = $8; $160 - $8 = $152
    ∴ The difference is $2 ($152 - 150)

42. **CORRECT ANSWER: D**
    $.25 x 3 = $.75. This would make it impossible to fill out the remainder of the $2.00 ($1.25) by dimes.

43. **CORRECT ANSWER: A**
    $\dfrac{10}{15} = \dfrac{2}{3} = .667$

44. **CORRECT ANSWER: D**
    3 ft. x 2/3 ft. (8 in.) x 1 ft. = 2 cu. ft.

45. **CORRECT ANSWER: A**
    288 = 2.88 hundreds
    ∴ $1250   2.88 = $3,600   Work   1250
                                       2.88
                                      10000
                                      10000
                                       2500
                                      3600.00

46. **CORRECT ANSWER: D**

Given	Years	Months	Days
	2014	2	12
	- 1994	3	15
Change to	2013	13	42
	- 1994	3	15
	19	10	27

47. **CORRECT ANSWER: B**

Given	Years	Months	Days
	2019	2	12
	- 1949	12	26
Change to	2018	13	42
	- 1949	12	26
	69	1	16

48. **CORRECT ANSWER: B**
    Given: $12.50 interest in 6 months at interest rate of 5% a year.
    This = $25.00 interest in one year
    $\therefore \$25.00 \div .05 =$

    $$\frac{\$25.00}{\frac{5}{100}} = \$25.00 \times \frac{100}{5} = \frac{\$25.00}{5} = \$500$$

49. **CORRECT ANSWER: A**
    4/5 (80%) x 35 = 28 (the number of items he must answer correctly)
    $\therefore$ 35 - 28 = 7 (the number of items he may miss)

50. **CORRECT ANSWER: A**
    Area of the entire rectangle - 15" x 16" = 90 sq. in.
    Area of the inner rectangle - 9" x 4" = 36 sq. in.
    $\therefore$ 90 sq. in. - 36 sq. in. = 54 sq. in. (area of the shaded portion of the rectangle)

ARITHMETICAL CONCEPTS AND EXERCISES

1. DECIMAL FRACTIONS AND EQUIVALENT DECIMAL FORMS

A decimal fraction is one whose denominator is 1, 10, 100, 1000, etc. For instance, 7/1, 3/10, 46/100, 7/1000, and 512/100 are decimal fractions. Each decimal fraction may be written as a decimal number and vice versa.

Example: 3/10 = 0.3 (three tenths)
Example: 46/100 = 0.46 (forty-six hundredths)
Example: 7/1000 = 0.007 (seven thousandths)
Example: 512/100 = 5.12 (five and twelve hundredths)

2. DECIMAL PLACE VALUE

The chart below shows the place values of decimals. Note the decimal fractions to the right of the decimal point.

1,000,000's	100,000's	10,000's	1,000's	100's	10's	1's	.	1/10's	1/100's	1/1000's	1/10000's	1/100000's	1/1000000's
millions	hundred-thousands	ten-thousands	thousands	hundreds	tens	ones	decimal point	tenths	hundredths	thousandths	ten-thousandths	hundred-thousandths	millionths

Thus, 316,000 represents three hundred-thousands plus one ten-thousand plus six thousands. Similarly, 0.05 represents five hundredths. The numeral 0.055 represents five hundredths plus five thousandths.

Sometimes, numerals that look different represent the same number. For example,

.33 = 3/10 + 3/100

.3300 = 3/10 + 3/100 + 0/1000 + 0/10000

In general, adding zeros to the right of the decimal point at the end of a numeral won't change the value: 0.5 = 0.50, 0.612 = 0.612000, etc. (But don't try this if the decimal point is absent! For example, 5 ≠ 50 and 612 ≠ 612,000)

EXERCISES

1. Write each of the following as a sum of decimal fractions: Example: 0.31 = 3/10 + 1/100

   A. 0.713   B. 0.0101   C. 0.16724

2. Write each of the following as a single decimal fraction: Example: 0.41 = 41/100

   A. 0.3   B. 0.03   C. 0.005   D. 0.13
   E. 1.65   F. 7   G. 37.126

3. ORDER OF DECIMAL NUMBERS

One of the great advantages of the decimal system is the ease with which two numbers can be compared; for example, which is larger: 37.39278 or 37.393841?

To answer a question like this, merely match the two numbers, decimal place by decimal place.

$$
\begin{array}{ccccccc}
3 & 7 \,. & 3 & 9 & 2 & 7 & 8 \\
\updownarrow & \updownarrow & \updownarrow & \updownarrow & \updownarrow & \updownarrow & \updownarrow \\
3 & 7 \,. & 3 & 9 & 3 & 8 & 4 \quad 1
\end{array}
$$

Here the second value of the two is larger. Both numbers contain 3 tens, 7 ones, 3 tenths and 9 hundredths. The second number, however, contains 3 thousandths whereas the first number contains only 2 thousandths. (No matter what digits appear to the right of the thousandths place, the second number will now always be larger than the first.)

Hence, you need only compare two numbers, decimal place by decimal place, from left to right, until you reach a place where the digits differ. The larger digit will belong to the larger number; for example, which is larger: 0.33 or 0.3321? Match up the first digit 3 in both numbers. So far the values are equal. Match up the second digit 3. The values are still equal. What in the first gets matched with the digit 2 in the second number? Recall that 0.33 = 0.3300 so

$$
\begin{array}{cccccc}
0 \,. & 3 & 3 & 0 & 0 \\
\updownarrow & \updownarrow & \updownarrow & \updownarrow & \updownarrow \\
0 \,. & 3 & 3 & 2 & 1
\end{array}
$$

the second number, 0.3321, is clearly larger than the first, 0.33.

EXERCISES

3. Identify the larger value.

   Example: 0.32 or 0.31. Answer: 0.32 because 0.32 contains 3 tenths and 2 hundredths, while 0.31 contains 3 tenths and only 1 hundredth. Note:

   $$\begin{matrix} 0 & 3 & 2 \\ \updownarrow & \updownarrow & \updownarrow \\ 0 & 3 & 1 \end{matrix}$$

   The value of 2 in the first number is larger than the value of 1 in the second number.

   Example: 0.32 or 0.317. Answer: 0.32 because, although both numbers contain 3 tenths, the first number contains more hundredths than the second. (Since the numbers differ at the second decimal place, we need not be concerned with the third or following decimal places.)

   Example: 0.31 or 0.317. Answer: 0.317 because 0.31 contains 3 tenths and 1 hudredth, but 0.317 contains 3 tenths, 1 hundredth, and 7 thousandths, or

   $0.31 = 3/10 + 1/100$ but $0.317 = 3/10 + 1/100 + 7/1000$

   A. 0.41689 or 0.4172*
   B. 3.716 or 3.7161
   C. 0.55 or 0.555
   D. .5 or .03
   E. 23.18 or 23.0971
   F. 14.386 or 14.00001
   G. 37.26 or 47.013

*NOTE: Some students feel that having many digits to the right of a decimal point makes a number small. This is an incorrect belief. It is the value of the digits that counts, not how many there are; for example:
   0.66666 is larger than 0.666,
   41.68888 is smaller than 41.7

4. Place in increasing order:

   A. 0.32, 0.3222, 0.370, 0.03
   B. 4.5, 4.05, 4.55, 4.3271
   C. 0.06, 0.31, 1.002, 0.56, 0.5

5. Identify three different numbers between 0.391 and 0.4

6. Which of the following lie between 0.6 and 0.41?
   0.06, 0.66, 0.5, 0.4444, 0.39, 0.599

7. An old document contains several six-digit decimal numbers. Unfortunately, some of the digits have faded and are indicated below by X's. Of the two values given, which number is the larger?

    A. 0.65X123 or 0.7XXXXXX
    B. 0.5X4000 or 0.6XX000
    C. 0.6X3124 or 0.6X4917
    D. 0.X5521X or 0.99131X

8. Which of the following lie between 1.003 and 1.2?
    1.125, 1.02, 1.00044, 1.111, 1.202

4. ADDING, SUBTRACTING, MULTIPLYING, AND DIVIDING DECIMALS

To add two or more decimal numerals, simply line up the decimal points and add. Thus, 3 + 4.68 + 7.1 becomes

$$\begin{array}{r} 3.0 \\ 4.68 \\ +7.1 \\ \hline 14.78 \end{array}$$

Subtraction is performed similarly.

Problem: Find 13.7 - 1.4
Solution:
$$\begin{array}{r} 13.7 \\ -1.4 \\ \hline 12.3 \end{array}$$

Problem: Find 1.2 - 0.687
Solution:
$$\begin{array}{r} 1.200 \\ -0.687 \\ \hline 0.513 \end{array}$$

To multiply two decimals, simply (a) multiply them as though they were whole numbers, (b) find the total number of digits to the right of the decimal point in the two numbers, (c) place the decimal point in your answer so that the number of digits to the decimal point's right is the number you found in (b).

Problem: Find 3.321 x 4.62
Solution:

    3.321   3 digits to right of decimal point
   x 4.62   2 digits to right of decimal point
    6642
   19926   Therefore, a total of 5 digit to right
  13284   of decimal point
 15.34302

Division of decimals is illustrated by the following two examples.

1. To see that 13.56 ÷ 12 = 1.13, simply proceed as though you are dividing whole numbers. However, note the placement of the decimal points.

Problem: Find 12)13.56

Solution:
```
        1.13
   12)13.56
      12
      ‾‾
       15
       12
       ‾‾
        36
        36
        ‾‾
         0
```

2. If the number you are dividing by is also a decimal, move the decimal points of both numerals before proceeding.

Problem: Find 56.58 ÷ 2.3

Solution: 56.58 ÷ 2.3   becomes

        2.3)56.58   and then

        2.3)56.5.8   or

        23)565.8   so

```
        24.6
   23) 565.8
       46
       ‾‾
       105
        92
        ‾‾
        138
        138
        ‾‾‾
          0
```

Thus, 56.58 ÷ 2.3 = 24.6

EXERCISES

9. Compute:

    A. 3.2 + 42.1
    B. 27.01 + 3.6
    C. 1.007 + 17 + 2.15
    D. 18.61 - 1.52
    E. 4 - 0.68
    F. 13.6 - 8.01

10. Find the product or quotient:

    A. 3.21 . 4.6*
    B. 18.6 . 1.021
    C. 68.64 ÷ 2.6

D. 174.512 ÷ 2.6
E. 14.5935 ÷ 4.7

NOTE: Like the symbol, x, the symbol, •, is sometimes used as the multiplicative symbol.

5. POWERS OF TEN, SCIENTIFIC NOTATION

The *powers of ten* are shown below:

...10^{-3} 10^{-2} 10^{-1} 10^0 10^1 10^2 10^3...
...0.001 0.01 0.1 1 10 100 1000...

Any decimal number may be multiplied by a power of ten. Simply look at the exponent of the power of ten; for example, the 3 of 10^3 or the -2 of 10^{-2}. That exponent tells you how many places to move the decimal point and the direction in which to move the decimal point in the number you are multiplying; thus, $324.213 \times 10^2 = 32421.3$. (The decimal moves two places to the right when multiplying by 102.) Also, $324.213 \times 10^{-2} = 3.24213$. (The decimal point moves two places to the left when multiplying by 10^{-2}.)

Scientific notation is the name given to a particularly succinct way of expressing unusually large or unusually small numbers; for example, 83,000,000 would be expressed as 8.3×10^7 in scientific notation.

A number expressed in scientific notation consists of one nonzero digit to the left of the decimal point and multiplication by some power of ten. For example:

Problem: Express in scientific notation: 461,000, 0.0018, 8,000,000 and 0.001001.

Solution:
$461,000 = 4.61 \times 10^5$
$0.0018 = 1.8 \times 10^{-3}$
$8,000,000 = 8.0 \times 10^6$
$0.001001 = 1.001 \times 10^{-3}$

EXERCISES

11. Express as a whole number or decimal:

    A. 10^2
    B. 10^4
    C. 10^{-5}
    D. 10^{-2}

12. Express as a power of ten:

    A. 1,000
    B. 0.001
    C. 100
    D. 0.000001

13. Express without using powers of ten:
    Example: $4.2 \times 10^3 = 4200$

    A. 3.608×10^7

B. 1.01×10^4
C. 3.0×10^2
D. 1.1721×10^{-6}

14. Express in scientific notation:

    A. 345,000,000
    B. 0.003
    C. 0.0001099
    D. 36

15. Express your answer as either an integer or a power of ten:

    A. 37 times what number equals 370,000?
    B. 10,000 is what number times 100?
    C. 10,000 is what number times 0.01?
    D. 13,000 times what number equals 13?
    E. 120 is what number times 1.2?

16. Fill in the blank with a power of ten:

    A. $3000 = 30 \times$ _____
    B. $30 = 3000 \times$ _____
    C. $3.45 = 3.45 \times$ _____
    D. $345 = 3.45 \times$ _____

6. FRACTIONS AS DECIMALS, ROUNDING DECIMALS

To write a fraction as a decimal, simply divide the numerator by the denominator.

Problem: Express as 1/4 as a decimal.

Solution:
```
      .25
   4)1.000
      8
      ‾‾
      20
      20
      ‾‾
       0
```

Since the division process may continue without end, it is sometimes necessary to approximate the answer by reporting only a few decimal places. This process is called *rounding*. Thus to convert 7/13 to a decimal, divide 13 into 7.0000 and obtain 0.5384.... If you round the answer to three decimal places, you will obtain 0.538. If the answer is rounded to the nearest hundredth (two decimal places), the answer would be 0.54. Rounding to the nearest tenth will give you 0.5.

To round to the nearest tenth, for example, look at the next digit to the right. If it is 4 or less, you simply drop all digits to the right of the tenths place. If it is 5 or more, you increase the tenths by one and then drop the digits to the right of that digit. Thus, rounded to the nearest tenth, 0.5321 becomes 0.5, whereas, 4.65182 becomes 4.7.

Rounding is not used solely for digits to the right of a decimal place. If 468,351 is rounded to, say, the nearest thousand, it becomes 468,000. Rounded to the nearest hundred, it becomes 468,400.*

*NOTE: Watch the wording when you are asked to round computations; for instance, *Round 4,168.3749 to the nearest hundredth* is not the same as *Round 4,168.3749 to the nearest hundred*. The answer to the first problem is 4,168.37, whereas the answer to the second problem is 4,200.

EXERCISES

17. Round to the nearest hundredth:

    A. 0.46802
    B. 0.5136
    C. 12.47491
    D. 1.725

18. Round to the nearest tenth:

    A. 317.64
    B. 34.550
    C. 1,435.0550
    D. 104.499

19. Round the numerals in item 18 above to the nearest ten.

20. Express as a decimal:

    A. 1/2
    B. 3/8
    C. 5/16

21. Express as a decimal rounded to the nearest thousandth:

    A. 1/7
    B. 9/16
    C. 3/17

7. ADDING, SUBTRACTING, MULTIPLYING, AND DIVIDING FRACTIONS

The easiest arithmetic operation to perform on fractions is multiplication. To multiply two fractions, simply multiply corresponding numerators and denominators.

Problem: Compute $\frac{3}{7} \times \frac{4}{11}$

Solution: $\frac{3}{7} \times \frac{4}{11} = \frac{12}{77}$

Problem: Compute 1/3 of 19

Solution: $\frac{1}{3}$ of $19 = \frac{1}{3} \times \frac{19}{1} = \frac{19}{3}$

Problem: Compute 1/2 of 18

Solution: $\frac{1}{2}$ of $18 = \frac{1}{2} \times \frac{18}{1} = \frac{18}{2} = 9$

To divide two fractions, use this rule: *invert and multiply.*

Problem: Compute $\dfrac{1}{3} \div \dfrac{3}{7}$

Solution: $\dfrac{1}{3} \div \dfrac{3}{7} = \dfrac{1}{3} \times \dfrac{7}{3} = \dfrac{7}{9}$

Problem: Compute $\dfrac{1}{7} \div 3$

Solution: $\dfrac{1}{7} \div 3 = \dfrac{1}{7} \div \dfrac{3}{1} = \dfrac{1}{7} \times \dfrac{1}{3} = \dfrac{1}{21}$

Adding and subtracting fractions is, in general, not as simple as multiplying and dividing fractions. However, fractions with equal denominators can be added or subtracted directly:

$\dfrac{1}{7} + \dfrac{3}{7} = \dfrac{4}{7}$** and $\dfrac{7}{8} - \dfrac{5}{8} = \dfrac{2}{8}$

**NOTE: To find the sum of two fractions, NEVER add denominators.

Thus, $\dfrac{1}{2} + \dfrac{1}{2} = \dfrac{2}{2} = 1, \dfrac{1}{2} + \dfrac{1}{2} \neq \dfrac{2}{4}$

Fractions with different denominators are more of a problem. In order to add or subtract, you must convert the fractions, so that the denominators are equal. This can be done by multiplying numerators and denoninators by the same whole number. In the first example below, the numerator and denominator of 1/2 are both multiplied by 3 in the first step.

Problem: $\dfrac{1}{6} + \dfrac{1}{2}$

Solution: $\dfrac{1}{6} + \dfrac{1}{2} = \dfrac{1}{6} + \dfrac{1}{2} \times \dfrac{3}{3}$ Therefore,

$= \dfrac{1}{6} + \dfrac{3}{6}$ and,

$= \dfrac{4}{6}$

Problem: $\dfrac{1}{15} + \dfrac{1}{5}$

Solution: $\dfrac{1}{15} + \dfrac{1}{5} = \dfrac{1}{15} + \dfrac{1}{5} \times \dfrac{3}{3}$ Therefore,

$= \dfrac{1}{15} + \dfrac{3}{15}$ and,

$= \dfrac{4}{15}$

Problem: $\dfrac{2}{7}+\dfrac{1}{3}$

Solution: $\dfrac{2}{7}+\dfrac{1}{3}=\dfrac{2}{7}\times\dfrac{3}{3}+\dfrac{1}{3}\times\dfrac{7}{7}$ yields

$$=\dfrac{6}{21}+\dfrac{7}{21}\quad\text{and,}$$

$$=\dfrac{13}{21}$$

Usually, fractions are reduced to lowest terms. Thus, 2/4 might be reduced to 1/2. To reduce 2/4 to lowest terms, divide both numerator and denominator by 2.

Here are three other examples.

Problem: Reduce these fractions: $\dfrac{21}{35},\dfrac{10}{80},\dfrac{63}{147}$

Solution: $\dfrac{21}{35}=\dfrac{3}{5}$ (numerator and denominator are divided by 7)

$\dfrac{10}{80}=\dfrac{1}{8}$ (numerator and denominator are divided by 10)

$\dfrac{63}{147}=\dfrac{3}{7}$ (numerator and denominator are divided by 21)

Finally, if you encounter fractions written in *mixed* form, you can easily convert them to pure fractional notation. For example, = 3/2. This is so because 1 = 2/2, so 1 1/2 = 1 +1/2 = 2/2 + 1/2 = 3/2. Likewise, 4 1/3 = 4 + 1/3 = 12/3 + 1/3 = 13/3*. You can also convert in the other direction. Start with 13/3 and, by dividing 3 into 13, you will see that it equals 4 1/3.

*NOTE: The general rule for such cases: $a\dfrac{b}{c}=\dfrac{a\times c+b}{c}$.

Thus, $4\ 1/3=\dfrac{4\times 3+1}{3}=\dfrac{13}{3}$

EXERCISES

22. Perform the indicated operations:

   A. $\dfrac{3}{7}\times\dfrac{5}{11}=$

   B. $\dfrac{1}{2}\times\dfrac{1}{7}=$

   C. $\dfrac{3}{5}\times 3=$

D. $\dfrac{3}{7} \div \dfrac{4}{11} =$

E. $15 \div \dfrac{1}{3} =$

F. $\dfrac{1}{7} + \dfrac{5}{7} =$

G. $\dfrac{3}{11} - \dfrac{2}{11} =$

H. $\dfrac{1}{10} + \dfrac{1}{5} =$

I. $\dfrac{1}{8} + \dfrac{5}{16} =$

J. $\dfrac{3}{7} + \dfrac{7}{15} =$

K. $\dfrac{4}{9} + \dfrac{1}{7} =$

L. $\dfrac{13}{5} - \dfrac{3}{2} =$

23. Reduce to lowest terms:

   A. $\dfrac{5}{15}$

   B. $\dfrac{4}{32}$

   C. $\dfrac{48}{208}$

   D. $\dfrac{154}{231}$

24. Add.

   Example: $3\dfrac{1}{3} + 4\dfrac{1}{4} = 7 + \dfrac{1}{3} + \dfrac{1}{4} = 7 + \dfrac{4}{12} + \dfrac{3}{12}$
   $= 7 + \dfrac{7}{12} = 7\dfrac{7}{12}$

   A. $3\dfrac{1}{2} + 4\dfrac{1}{3}$

   B. $7\dfrac{2}{5} + 8\dfrac{1}{3}$

C. $5\frac{4}{5} + 1\frac{1}{4}$

8. ORDER AMONG FRACTIONS

How can you tell which of two fractions is larger? Sometimes little work is required when you can compare both fractions to a third fraction. We know, for example, that 5/8 is larger than 3/10 because 5/8 is larger than 1/2, whereas 3/10 is smaller than 1/2.

For more difficult comparisons, we can convert both fractions to decimal form and then compare the decimals. Thus, to compare 5/8 and 3/5, we might divide numerators by denominators, converting both to decimals. We would find that 5/8 = 0.625 and 3/5 = 0.6. Since 0.625 is larger than 0.6, it follows that 5/8 is larger than 3/5.

Of course, if both fractions have the same denominator, you can see at once which is larger. Obviously, 4/7 is larger than 3/7.

EXERCISES

25. Which is larger? 8/21 or 3/8?

26. Which is larger?

    A. $\frac{4}{7}$ or $\frac{3}{5}$?

    B. $\frac{4}{17}$ or $\frac{5}{21}$?

    C. $\frac{13}{15}$ or $\frac{8}{9}$?

27. Arrange in increasing order.

    A. $0.5, \frac{4}{7}, \frac{1}{3}, \frac{7}{17}, \frac{9}{19}, \frac{13}{23}$

    B. $\frac{9}{19}, 0.45, \frac{2}{5}, \frac{17}{40}, \frac{4}{9}$

28. Which values lie between 1/2 and 2/3 ?

    $\frac{3}{5}, \frac{5}{8}, 0.72, 0.05, \frac{5}{11}$

9. MEANING OF *PERCENT*

The word *percent* and the symbol % mean *per hundred*. Thus, since 25/100 means 25 per hundred, we can write 25/100 = 25%. Likewise, 13/100 = 13% and 7/100 = 7%.

To say, *All items on display are marked down 25%* means that each item has its price reduced by 25/100 = 1/4.

You will get 50% better gas mileage with this model car indicates that your mileage will go up by 50/100 = 1/2 of what it might otherwise be.

A percent can be written in decimal form. Simply move the decimal point two places to the left.

$$50\% = 0.50$$
$$25\% = 0.25$$
$$133\% = 1.33$$

Percents may also be written as fractions:

$$50\% = 1/2$$
$$75\% = 3/4$$
$$125\% = 1\frac{1}{4}$$

EXERCISES

29. Write as a fraction.

    A. 20%
    B. 75%
    C. 9%

30. Write as a decimal.

    A. 15%
    B. 246%
    C. 30%
    D. 9%
    E. 100%
    F. 1%

31. Compute.
    Example: 45% of 200 = 0.45 x 200 = 90.00

    A. 35% of 300
    B. 8% of $81.50
    C. 17% of $63

32. Place in increasing order:

    $$\frac{1}{2}, \frac{3}{7}, 42\%, 56\%, \frac{3}{8}, 100\%$$

33. Change the percents to fractions and solve.

    A. What is 50% of 80?
    B. What is 25% of 80?
    C. What is 10% of 80?
    D. What is 42% of 100?

10. DECIMALS AND FRACTIONS AS PERCENTS

Since a percent can be expressed as a decimal by moving the decimal point two places to the left, one can reverse the process to express a decimal as percent. Move the decimal point two places to the right to convert a decimal to a percent.

Example:
A. $0.50 = 50\%$
B. $0.417 = 41.7\%$
C. $3 = 300\%$

Convert fractions to percents by converting the fraction to a decimal, then changing the decimal to a percent. Thus, by dividing 7.000 by 13, we can convert 7/13 into 0.538461. Round off the answer to three decimal places, for example, then move the decimal point two places to the right: $0.538 = 53.8\%$. Hence, 7/13 is approximately 53.8%

Of course, if you have a fraction that has, or can easily be made to have, a denominator of 100, converting to a percent is easy.

Problem: Convert the following to percents:

A. $\dfrac{20}{100}$

B. $\dfrac{8}{100}$

C. $\dfrac{1}{2}$

D. $\dfrac{1}{5}$

E. $2\dfrac{1}{4}$

Solution:

A. $\dfrac{20}{100} = 20\%$

B. $\dfrac{8}{100} = 8\%$

C. $\dfrac{1}{2} = \dfrac{50}{100} = 50\%$

D. $\dfrac{1}{5} = \dfrac{20}{100} = 20\%$

E. $2\dfrac{1}{4} = 2 + \dfrac{25}{100} = \dfrac{200}{100} + \dfrac{25}{100} = \dfrac{225}{100} = 225\%$

EXERCISES

34. Express as percents

   A. 0.13
   B. 3.17
   C. 0.065

35. Express as percents.

   A. 1/10
   B. 3/4
   C. 51/100
   D. 2/5
   E. 1

36. Express as percents.

   A. 6/13
   B. 1/3
   C. 1/8
   D. 9/4

11. ESTIMATING THE OUTCOMES OF COMPUTATIONS

The art of estimating depends on rounding off numbers involved in computations so that you can calculate an approximate result mentally. Thus, $32.08 - $14.86 becomes $32 - $15 or approximately $17.

Estimation can involve not only decimal numerals, but fractions and percents as well. Thus, 3 5/8 + 2 1/4 could be rounded to 4 + 2 and estimated as 6. Round 3 5/8 up to 4; round to 2; and note that 4+2=6.

Suppose your dinner bill is $48.44 and you want to leave a 15% tip; approximately how much is 15% of $48.44? Do some mental estimation: 10% of $48.44 becomes 10% of $48. You know that 10% of anything can be found by simply moving the decimal point one digit to the left. So, 10% of $48.00 is $4.80; therefore, 5% of $48.00 must be 1/2 of $4.80 or $2.40. Since $4.80 (10% of 48)+ $2.40(5% of 48) is about $7, your tip is roughly $7.

EXERCISES

37. What whole number is closest to the following?

   A. 4.37
   B. 0.78
   C. 36.95

38. What multiple of 10 is closest to the following?

   A. 39.7
   B. 42.68
   C. 386.71

39. Estimate mentally:
    - A. $30 - $5.95
    - B. 1/2 of $29.65
    - C. 3 3/4 + 2 1/8 + 1 1/16
    - D. 5% of 86.21
    - E. 50% of $89.20
    - F. 6/7 + 10/11
    - G. 7 1/2 % of $19.86
    - H. 32.61 x 48
    - I. 4 1/3 x 91

40. John bought 3 textbooks that cost $14.95, $7.15, and $19.78. About how much will remain from the $50 that John brought with him?

41. You have a map of coastal Maine that reads *1 inch equals approximately 2.3 miles.* You estimate the distance from Wells to Saco as a little over 6 inches. Estimate the distance in miles.

42. A student has quiz grades of 86, 78, 52, 92. Estimate the student's average.

KEY (CORRECT ANSWERS)

1. A. $\dfrac{7}{10} + \dfrac{1}{100} + \dfrac{3}{1000}$

   B. $\dfrac{1}{100} + \dfrac{1}{10000}$ or $\dfrac{0}{10} + \dfrac{1}{100} + \dfrac{0}{1000} + \dfrac{1}{10000}$

   C. $\dfrac{1}{10} + \dfrac{6}{100} + \dfrac{7}{1000} + \dfrac{2}{10000} + \dfrac{4}{100000}$

2. A. $\dfrac{3}{10}$

   B. $\dfrac{3}{100}$

   C. $\dfrac{5}{1000}$

   D. $\dfrac{13}{100}$

   E. $\dfrac{165}{100}$

   F. $\dfrac{7}{1}$

   G. $\dfrac{37126}{1000}$

3. A. 0.4172 because 7/1000 is larger than 6/1000
   B. 3.7161 because 1/10000 is larger than 0/10000
   C. 0.555 because 5/1000 is larger than 0/1000
   D. 0.5 because 5/10 is larger than 0/10
   E. 23.18 because 1/10 is larger than 0/10
   F. 14.386 because 3/10 is larger than 0/10
   G. 47.013 because 4 tens is larger than 3 tens

4. A. 0.03, 0.32, 0.3222, 0.370
   B. 4.05, 4.3271, 4.5, 4.55
   C. 0.06, 0.31, 0.5, 0.56, 1.002

5. Any three decimals which start out 0.39...and where the digit to the right of the 9 is 1 or greater. (There may be any number of digits to the right of the decimal point, but it's only the first three which determine the correct answer.)

6. 0.5, 0.4444, and 0.599

7. A. 0.7XXXXX
    B. 0.6XX000
    C. You cannot tell. For example, the numbers might be 0.653124 and 0.654917, in which case the second is larger. But the numbers could be 0.653124 and 0.644917, in which case the first is larger.
    D. 0.99131X

8. 1.125, 1.02, 1.111

9. A. 45.3
    B. 30.61
    C. 20.157
    D. 17.09
    E. 4.00 - 0.68 = 3.32
    F. 13.60 - 8.01 = 5.59

10. A. 14.766
    B. 18.9906
    C. 26.4
    D. 67.12
    E. 3.105

11. A. $10^2 = 100$
    B. $10^4 = 10{,}000$
    C. $10^{-5} = 0.00001$
    D. $10^{-2} = 0.01$

12. A. $1000 = 10^3$
    B. $0.001 = 10^{-3}$
    C. $100 = 10^2$
    D. $0.000001 = 10^{-6}$

13. A. 36,080,000
    B. 10,100
    C. 300
    D. 0.0000011721

14. A. 3.45×10^8
    B. 3×10^{-3}
    C. 1.099×10^{-4}
    D. 3.6×10

15. A. 10,000 or 10^4
    B. 100 or 10^2
    C. 1,000,000 or 10^6
    D. 0.001 or 10^{-3}
    E. 100 or 10^2

16. A. 10^2
    B. 10^{-2}
    C. 10
    D. 10^2

17. A. 0.47
    A. 0.51
    B. 12.47
    C. 1.73

18. A. 317.6
    B. 34.6
    C. 1435.1
    D. 104.5

19. A. 320
    B. 30
    C. 1440
    D. 100

20. A. 0.5
    B. 0.375
    C. 0.3125

21. A. 0.143
    A. 0.563
    B. 0.176

22. A. 15/77
    B. 1/14
    C. 9/5
    D. 33/28
    E. 45/1=45
    F. 6/7
    G. 1/11
    H. 3/10
    I. 7/16
    J. 94/105
    K. 37/63
    L. 11/10

23. A. 1/3
    B. 1/8
    C. 3/13
    D. 2/3

24. A. 7 5/6
    B. 15 11/15
    C. $5\dfrac{4}{5}+1\dfrac{1}{4}=6+\dfrac{4}{5}+\dfrac{1}{4}=6+\dfrac{16+5}{20}=6+\dfrac{21}{20}=6+1+\dfrac{1}{20}=7\dfrac{1}{20}$

25. We convert both to decimals by the long division process.
8/21 = 0.380...and 3/8 = 0.375.... Thus we can see by comparing the first two digits to the right of the decimal point that 8/21 is larger.

26. A. 3/5
B. 5/21
C. 8/9

27. A. $\frac{1}{3}(.33), \frac{7}{17}(.41), \frac{9}{19}(.47), 0.5, \frac{13}{23}(.56), \frac{4}{7}(.57)$

B. $\frac{2}{5}(.40), \frac{17}{40}(.43), \frac{4}{9}(.44), 0.45, \frac{9}{19}(.47)$

28. 3/5, 5/8

29. A. $\frac{20}{100} = \frac{1}{5}$

B. $\frac{75}{100} = \frac{3}{4}$

C. $\frac{9}{100}$

30. A. 0.15
B. 2.46
C. 0.30
D. 0.09
E. 1.00
F. 0.01

31. A. 0.35 x 300 = 105
B. 0.08 x $81.50 = $6.52
C. 0.17 x 63 = 10.71

32. $\frac{3}{8}(.38), 42\%(.42), \frac{3}{7}(.43), \frac{1}{2}(.50), 56\%(.56), 100\%(1.00)$

33. A. 40
B. 20
C. 8
D. 42

34. A. 13%
B. 317%
C. 6.5%

35. A. 1/10 = 10/100 = 10%
    B. 3/4 = 75/100 = 75%
    C. 51%
    D. 2/5 = 40/100 = 40%
    E. 1 = 100/100%

36. A. 6/13 = 0.4651... and is approximately 46.2%
    B. 1/3 = 0.3333... and is approximately 33.3%
       Some people prefer the exact answer 1/3 = 33 1/3%
    C. 1/8 = 0.125 = 12.5%
    D. 9/4 = 2.25 = 225%

37. A. 4
    B. 1
    C. 37

38. A. 40
    B. 40
    C. 390

39. A. $30 - $6 = $24
    B. 1/2 of $30 = $15
    C. 7
    D. 10% of 86 is 8.6, so 5% is 4.3. (You might call it 4.)
    E. 50% of $90 = $45
    F. 2
    G. 7% of $20 is $1.40 (0.07 X 20 = 1.40)
       8% of $20 is $1.60. So is about $1.50
    H. 30 x 50 = 1500
    I. $4\frac{1}{3} \times 90 = (4 \times 90) + (\frac{1}{3} \times 90) = 360 + 30 = 390$

40. $15 + $7 + $20 = $42. About $8 will be left.

41. 6 x 2.3 = (6x2) + (6x0.3) = 12+2 (since 6x0.3 = 1.8) = 14 miles

42. 86 + 92 + 78 + 52 roughly equal 90 + 90 + 80 + 50 = 310. The average would be approximately 320/4 = 80. The average should be slightly less than 80, perhaps 77 or 78.

www.ingramcontent.com/pod-product-compliance
Lightning Source LLC
Chambersburg PA
CBHW082125230426
43671CB00015B/2811